# ENVIRONMENTAL STRATEGY AND SUSTAINABLE DEVELOPMENT

This radical new book represents an attempt to forward the debate over environmental strategy in business. It is argued that traditional approaches to environmental management cannot deliver sustainability and this book therefore outlines where we must go next in order to avoid the path towards self-destruction.

Central to this book is the concept of sustainable development dealt with in a postmodern framework. Ethical issues are placed firmly on the business agenda; what is required is a change in ideology, an acceptance by industry of its ethical and social responsibilities.

At the core of the book, a clear distinction is made between strategies associated with environmental management, ecological management and sustainable development. The approach taken is that environmental management incorporates all the mainstream (inadequate) approaches to environmental improvement that we have seen to date. Ecological management goes further than that in introducing elements of deep ecology into business strategy. Strategies associated with sustainability incorporate ecological strategy but go further in considering the organisation's role in respect of equity, equality, and futurity.

Richard Welford challenges by looking forward to what is possible through commitment, creativity and a challenge to conservatism. In developing the notion of the transcendent organisation, *Environmental Strategy and Sustainable Development* ends by building a radical business agenda for the future.

**Richard Welford** is Professor of Business Economics at the University of Huddersfield. He is one of the leading experts on environmental strategy for business.

# ENVIRONMENTAL STRATEGY AND SUSTAINABLE DEVELOPMENT

The corporate challenge for the
twenty-first century

*Richard Welford*

London and New York

First published 1995
by Routledge
11 New Fetter Lane, London EC4P 4EE

Simultaneously published in the USA and Canada
by Routledge
29 West 35th Street, New York, NY 10001

© 1995 Richard Welford

Phototypeset in Garamond by Intype, London
Printed in Great Britain by
Biddles Ltd, Guildford and King's Lynn

*British Library Cataloging in Publication Data*
A catalogue record for this book is available from the British Library

ISBN 0–415–10551–X (hbk)
ISBN 0–415–10552–8 (pbk)

*Library of Congress Cataloging in Publication Data*
Welford, Richard, 1960–
Environmental strategy and sustainable development/the corporate
challenge for the 21st century/Richard Welford.
p.   cm.
Includes index.   *Po 5968*
ISBN 0–415–10551–X. — ISBN 0–415–10552–8 (pbk.)
1. Industrial management—Environmental aspects.   2. Sustainable
development—Moral and ethical aspects.   3. Social responsibility of
business.   I. Title.
HD69.P6W45   1995
658.4′08—dc20
94—11957
CIP

On 21 February 1994 I was close to completing the manuscript for this book. On that day the British House of Commons refused to lower the age of consent for gay men to 16, which would have brought it into line with the heterosexual age of consent.

That event merely demonstrates that we continue to live in a society of inequity and inequality and, until we rectify that situation, we have no right to consider ourselves civilised.

This book is dedicated to all those people who strive to bring about a world which is equitable and sustainable. Such a world is achievable: it simply requires commitment, creativity and a challenge to conservative ideologies.

# CONTENTS

# FIGURES

# TABLES

# PREFACE

This book represents an attempt to move forward the debate over environmental strategy in business. In the past I have written texts which map out traditional approaches to environmental management. A minority of firms have put such strategies in place with mixed results. But traditional approaches to environmental management systems and environmental auditing will not deliver sustainability. They take us perhaps 20 per cent of the way there. This book therefore contributes to the debate over where to go next. Although it is recognised that the majority of businesses are still doing very little to improve environmental performance, now is the time to set off on a debate about strategies appropriate to the twenty-first century.

The first two chapters of this book set the scene for that which is to come. Specifically in chapter 1 we deal with the concept of sustainable development. This is perhaps the most important concept and challenge facing every one of us in the world today. It is set firmly within a postmodern paradigm which argues that we should distance ourselves from assumptions of unity and therefore question the generic codes of conduct which make up contemporary corporate environmental philosophy. It is argued that there is no single ideology of universal relevance and culture becomes divided into discrete spheres. This being the case, we are forced to challenge simple categorisations, structures and codes which purport to move us towards sustainability.

Chapter 2 deals with business ethics and ethical approaches to environmental strategy. In identifying the many unethical approaches taken to the environment in the last decades, it is argued that what is required is a thorough re-examination of business ethics within any organisation and a change in ideology towards an acceptance by industry of its ethical and social responsibilities.

In chapters 3 to 5 and at the core of this book, a clear distinction is made between strategies associated with environmental management, ecological management and sustainable development. The approach taken here is that environmental management incorporates all the mainstream approaches to environmental improvement that we have seen to date. It encompasses an approach to environmental improvement based on the establishment and operation of environmental management systems. Ecological management, it is argued, goes further than that in introducing elements of deep ecology into business strategy. Thus more emphasis is placed on life cycle assessment, a dynamic (rather than static) approach to auditing and a greater respect for ecosystems and biodiversity. Strategies associated with sustainability incorporate ecological strategy but go further in considering the organisation's role in respect of equity and futurity.

Culture change is one of the most powerful tools able to change the shape, organisation and values of a business. In chapter 6 a detailed examination is made of culture change strategies and a model for the implementation of values in accordance with sustainable development is provided. This chapter draws significantly on the excellent research work of David Jones and I would wish to pay tribute to his efforts in helping me to write this chapter.

In chapter 7 we return to the important consideration of business ethics and environmental strategy in a consideration of green marketing and eco-labelling. It is argued that green marketing represents a discrete shift away from the more unethical and spurious green marketing strategies so common to date. Moreover it is suggested that it is not enough to promote products alone and any organisation needs to examine its overall impact on and commitment to the environment. The green company will also be a campaigning company and be committed to spreading an ethical communication message about sustainable development. Third party eco-labelling schemes can be part of the environmental message but it is argued in this chapter that as a minimum a full product assessment approach should be introduced which considers wider aspects of ecological issues including animal rights.

Global change to bring about a sustainable future requires local action and the penultimate chapter of this book examines the issues of regionalism and bioregionalism. Two models are outlined, the first, the traditional regional environmental management system approach and the second, a more radical approach based on the concept of bioregionalism. These approaches are not mutually exclusive and the first approach naturally leads on to the second. In this chapter we revisit the concept of postmodernism in arguing that the bioregional approach is fully consistent with the changes taking place in the postmodern society.

The last chapter looks forward at what is possible with commitment, creativity and a challenge to conservatism. In developing the notion of the transcendent organisation it is possible to build a radical business agenda for the future. This agenda for change is achievable and summarises the actions which have been advocated throughout the book. Those with a flexible intellect and a creative mind will find it thought provoking and stimulating. Others will undoubtedly brand it as the machinations of an out of touch academic.

But out of touch I am not. I have a great deal of experience in putting traditional forms of environmental management into businesses and that has made me realise that they are inadequate. I understand that the ecological signs around us point to a path towards self-destruction. I understand what it is not to fit into mainstream society and to be discriminated against. I have seen what it is like when we torture, maim and kill animals in the name of human progress. I wonder how many managers have even thought about the issues implicit in my experiences. What I therefore advocate is not an ill-defined policy of 'back to basics' associated with so many conservative thinkers, but a radical policy of grasping the future and controlling it to bring about an equitable and sustainable twenty-first century.

I am indebted to so many people in writing this book. Without his love and support, life would be less rich and therefore I pay tribute to Chris Maddison for putting up with my bad temper. For their help, advice and stimulation in writing this book I must thank David Wheeler and his staff at The Body Shop, Mark Shayler, John Dodge, David Jones, Donal O'Laoire and Nigel Roome. I am, of course, responsible for the ultimate content and views expressed in this text.

Richard Welford

# 1

# SUSTAINABLE DEVELOPMENT AND POSTMODERNISM

## INTRODUCTION

There can be little doubt that the waves of environmental concern which we have seen over the last thirty years have oscillated around an upward trend. In the 1990s those real concerns have become so great that legislators, regulators, policy makers and some polluters have given environmental considerations their proper place amongst all the other competing objectives of a modern pluralist society. It is difficult to assess precisely when the new environmental emphasis which we observe in contemporary society first began. It was clearly a phenomenon of the 1960s and many people have dated the rise of the environmental movement at 1962, the first publication of Rachel Carson's book entitled *Silent Spring*. In that book she writes:

For the first time in the history of the world, every human being is now subjected to contact with dangerous chemicals, from the moment of conception until death. In the less than two decades of their use, the synthetic pesticides have been so thoroughly distributed throughout the animate and inanimate world that they occur virtually everywhere. They have been recovered from most of the major river systems and even from the streams of groundwater flowing unseen through the earth. Residues of these chemicals linger in soil to which they may have been applied a dozen years before. They have entered and lodged in the bodies of fish, birds, reptiles, and domestic and wild animals so universally that scientists carrying on animal experiments find it almost impossible to locate subjects free from such contamination. They have been found in fish in remote mountain lakes, in earthworms burrowing in soil, in the eggs of birds – and in man himself. For these chemicals are now stored in the vast majority of human beings, regardless of age. They occur in the mother's milk, and probably in the tissues of the unborn child.

(Carson, 1965: 31)

Very little has changed in the more than two decades since such views were first expressed. Indeed were such a passage to be written today, few would refute it. Moreover, the situation has probably been compounded many fold such that we now face a real crisis which may ultimately affect the very existence of human life on the planet and the planet itself.

This book is unashamedly about reform, but it is argued throughout that that reform must be more radical than the piece-meal approaches that we have seen to date. Some may still argue that reformist efforts merely forestall the impending collapse of the industrial economies, a collapse which may need to occur before the real work of reconstruction can begin (Tokars, 1987). That may indeed be the case, but this book argues that there are significant reforms which we should adopt that may avoid this impending doom. Ostensibly that reform has to revolve around the fundamental ways in which we do business, in which the capitalist system forces businesses to operate and in the organisation of enterprises which are responsible for so much damage to date. The view of authors such as Elkington and Burke (1987) who we might consider as representative of marginalist reformers are nevertheless rejected. This is because they argue that:

> what we are seeing is the emergence of a new age of capitalism, appropriate to a new millennium, in which the boundary between corporate and human values is beginning to dissolve. It is now clear from the results who won the nineteenth-century argument about capital and labour. Socialism, as an economic theory, though not as a moral crusade, is dead. The argument is about what kind of capitalism we want.

(Elkington and Burke, 1987: 250)

Such an approach represents the view that we can tinker with the system and that capitalism is not fundamentally flawed. It suggests that we can introduce new 'eco-friendly' codes of conduct and legislation and that we can use the price mechanism to bring about desired change. Nowhere do marginalist reformers (who are often

2

more interested in exploiting the environment for personal gain) consider the dominant ideology of present forms of capitalism and they lack the imagination and creativity to develop the real strategies which will bring about the fundamental change which is needed. Theirs is a view which sees 'business as usual' supplemented by marginal changes in business operations to bring about incremental environmental improvement. But 'business as usual', no matter the extent to which that integrates environmental costs, is still largely alien to the sustainability of the planet. We need to recognise that the issues surrounding human life and economic activity are an interdependent part of wider ecological processes that sustain life on earth. We must operate within those ecological processes or they will, in turn, bring about the demise of those very issues. That requires fundamental reforms of the structures and processes which have caused the problem in the first place. That means finding new ways of doing business, of emancipating workers, of protecting the Third World and indigenous populations, and of sustaining all other life forms on the planet. The views of marginalist reformers seem not to fit into such an ethic. They merely scratch the surface of the problem and quickly paper over the cracks with industry-centred and profit-centred solutions. It should be stressed at this stage, however, that there is no suggestion that we need to operate wholly outside the free-market economy, only that the dominant ideology of capitalism based on the exploitation of valuable resources (including people) needs to be fundamentally reassessed.

What is being advocated in the chapters that follow may therefore seem controversial to some but there is a fundamental need to examine and redefine some of the sacred tenets of traditional economic thought. We cannot rely on established structures, technology and science to bring about real change. They have not done so to date. There is a need for a more radical rethink of many of the issues which face society and as part of that we need to think carefully about enterprise culture. What nobody can provide, however, is a formula for the way in which societies must operate into the future. When Karl Marx was once asked to describe what a communist society would look like, he replied that he could not write recipes for the cookshops of the future. We can, however, point to the inadequacies of current environmental strategies and point to the directions in which organisations must tread.

One thing is sure, however, and that is that we can no longer rely on science and technology to dig us out of the holes which we have created. When in 1798 Thomas Malthus warned that the population was growing so fast that it would eventually outstrip food supply, technology rescued us in the form of fertilisers and refrigeration. Now as the population rises exponentially Malthusian voices are raised again but their faith in the technological fix has deserted them. Moreover, the science and technology which initially provided deliverance now leads to sick plants with inadequate resistance to pests, to water contaminated by the pesticides which were supposed to put that problem right, and to desertification and erosion. Nevertheless this book does not represent a doctrine of despair. It does, however, encourage the reader to think more widely about the environmental strategies which we need to pursue in order to bring about an end to the mounting degradation of the planet.

## THE ENVIRONMENTAL CHALLENGE AND BUSINESS STRATEGY

We have established that environmental issues are not new; they have been a matter of public concern for over a quarter of a century. As scientific and technical knowledge relating to the cause and effect of environmental damage has become more complete, the pressure to change the ways in which industry behaves has increased. Individuals are also changing their patterns of behaviour and industry is having to respond to the seemingly endless demands of the modern, environmentally aware consumer.

In its early stages, the environmental debate in industry was largely one of rhetoric rather than action. More recently, businesses have recognised the need to improve their environmental performance but we have still not seen any radical shift in business practices which are capable of bringing about a lasting reversal of trends towards environmental destruction. While it is difficult for industry to refute the general need for environmental protection, their response has been piecemeal, adopting bolt-on strategies aimed at fine-tuning their environmental performance within the traditional constraints imposed by a traditional capitalist society. To date there have been a lot of publications aimed at telling businesses how they can achieve a measure of environmental improvement, but rather less on posing industry with a real challenge to change the very way in which it operates which will lead

4

to real progress. There is a need to develop practical solutions to meet the environmental challenge. However, it must be recognised that those solutions mean re-evaluating the very basis on which we do business.

Traditionally the view of the corporate world has been based on the idea that the investments and innovations of industry drive economic growth and satisfy the demands of the consumer. However in doing so, be it because of the resources that they consume, the processes that they apply or the products that they manufacture, business activity has become a major contributor to environmental destruction (Welford and Gouldson, 1993). Many reformists have argued that we need to find new technologies and to develop more efficient methods of production. But the very basis of that argument needs to be examined carefully. Growth can no longer be a sole objective which stands alone and pays no heed to its environmental consequences now and into the future. Growth is only justifiable if it is associated with development which in itself needs to concentrate more directly on equity. We know that the technological solution is insufficient in itself and we cannot assume that science and technology will cure the wrongs of the past and provide a new growth path. There is a need for a change in attitudes towards both consumption and production. Moreover, there is a need to look closely at the ethics of business and to discover new forms of industrial organisation and culture which, whilst existing in a broad free market framework with due regulation, promote development and equity into the future.

For a long time now neo-classical economists have told us that if harnessed correctly, the market mechanism can be utilised to develop the solutions which are so vital if the environment is to be protected. But the free market, to date, has failed to bring about equitable distributions of income, it has failed to protect the Third World and it has done little to protect the planet. Moreover, the market solution depends on cooperation between government, which must provide fiscal incentives for environmental improvement, industry and consumers. But each of these agencies have competing objectives and often competing values. In particular, industry, to date, has been driven by profitability and whilst that profitability might be seen as vital to economic growth we should begin to demand that industry puts ethical objectives, such as environmental improvement and sustainable development, into its strategic plan. Reliance on the market mechanism alone is likely to be insufficient to bring about real improvement. That is not to suggest that it has no role, but that it needs to be supplemented by changes in corporate culture based on a commitment to see long term environmental improvement and equitable development. These are the challenges for industry posed by the concept of sustainable development – a concept which, to date, industry has paid mere lip-service to.

## SUSTAINABLE DEVELOPMENT

The continuing ability of the environment to supply raw materials and assimilate waste while maintaining biodiversity and quality of life is being increasingly undermined. If growth and development are to take on new responsible paths we have to find a way of doing it that will not further degrade the environment in which we live. In its simplest form, sustainable development is defined as development that meets the needs of the present generation without compromising the ability of future generations to meet their own needs (World Commission on Environment and Development, 1987). Such a simple statement has profound implications. It implies that, as a minimum, all human activity must refrain from causing any degree of permanent damage through its consumption of environmental resources.

As an ultimate objective, the concept of sustainability is immensely valuable. However, strategies are needed to translate conceptual theories into practical reality. This requires a more radical assessment of environmental strategy than we have seen to date. The challenge that faces the economic system is how to continue to fulfil its vital role within modern society whilst ensuring sustainability. The emphasis to date has been on piecemeal moves towards sustainability and although this move is in the right direction, it lacks the sense of urgency and commitment which is required. There is a need to carefully assess how development can be made sustainable and this implies acceptance of the view that not all growth and development will be good. We must accept that sustainability is not something that will be achieved overnight, but in the longer term, entire economies and individual businesses need to look towards a new type of development and growth. This, in turn, requires them to look at their own ethics, their objectives and their own forms of organisation, corporate culture and communication.

One major obstacle preventing sustainability from being achieved is the overall level of consumption experienced in the Western world. Consumers who are relatively wealthy seem reluctant to significantly reduce their own levels of consumption. Whilst increasingly governments are adopting economic instruments such as taxes, subsidies and product labelling schemes to reduce and channel consumption towards more environmentally friendly alternatives, there is also a need for education amongst consumers. In addition, though, industry has a role to play in educating their customers and suppliers and all businesses must be encouraged to further increase their own internal environmental efficiency by reassessing the very ways in which they do business and measuring and assessing their environmental performance. We return to this issue later in the chapter.

The fact which lies behind the concept of sustainable development is that there is a trade-off between continuous economic growth and the sustainability of the environment. Over time, through greater and greater exploitation, growth causes pollution and atmospheric damage, disrupts traditional ways of living (particularly in the Third World), destroys ecosystems and feeds more and more power into oligopolistic industrial structures. The concept of sustainable development stresses the interdependence between economic growth and environmental quality, but it also goes further in demonstrating that the future is uncertain unless we can deal with issues of equity and inequality throughout the whole world. It is possible to make development and environmental protection compatible and to begin to deal with the problems caused by a lack of consideration of equity issues, by following sustainable strategies and by not developing the particular areas of economic activity that are most damaging to the environment and its inhabitants.

The Brundtland Report, commissioned by the United Nations to examine long term environmental strategies, argued that economic development and environmental protection could be made compatible, but that this would require quite radical changes in economic practices throughout the world. Mass consumption is not possible indefinitely and if society today acts as if all non-renewable resources are plentiful, eventually there will be nothing left for the future. But more importantly than that, mass consumption may cause such irreparable damage that humans may not even be able to live on the planet in the future.

Sustainable development is made up of three closely connected issues and each one of these needs to be addressed by industry. Firstly, the environment must be valued as an integral part of the economic process and not treated as a free good. The environmental stock has to be protected and this implies minimal use of non-renewable resources and minimal emission of pollutants. Ecosystems have to be protected so the loss of plant and animal species has to be avoided.

Secondly there is a need to deal with the issue of equity. One of the biggest threats facing the world is that the developing countries want to grow rapidly to achieve the same standards of living as those in the West. That in itself would cause major environmental degradation if it were modelled on the same sort of growth experienced in post-war Europe. There therefore needs to be a greater degree of equity and the key issue of poverty has to be addressed. But equity applies not only to relationships between the First and Third Worlds, but also within countries between people. A major source of inequality exists between those who are employed and unemployed and this must also be tackled within the context of sustainability.

Thirdly, sustainable development requires that society, businesses and individuals operate on a different time scale than currently operates in the economy. This is the issue of futurity. Whilst companies commonly operate under competitive pressures to achieve short run gains, long term environmental protection is often compromised. To ensure that longer term, inter-generational considerations are observed, longer planning horizons need to be adopted and business policy needs to be proactive rather than reactive.

The Brundtland Report concludes that these three conditions are not being met. The industrialised world has already used much of the planet's ecological capital and many of the development paths of the industrialised nations are clearly unsustainable. Non-renewable resources are being depleted, while renewable resources such as soil, water and the atmosphere are being degraded. This has been caused by economic development but in time will undermine the very foundations of that development.

The Brundtland Report calls for growth which is environmentally and socially sustainable rather than the current situation of unplanned, undifferentiated growth. This means reconsidering the current measures of growth, such as gross national product (GNP), which fail to take account of environmental debits like pollution or the depletion of the natural capital stock. Whilst concern about the depletion of materials and energy resources has diminished since the 1970s there is nevertheless now concern surrounding the environment's capacity to act as a sink for waste. For example, bringing developing countries' standards of living up to the level of the developing world's would mean an unsustainable increase in the consumption and generation of energy. Using present energy generation methods the planet could not cope with the impact of sulphur dioxide and carbon dioxide emissions and the acidification and global warming of the environment which would be consequential.

It seems clear therefore that industry must seek to provide the services demanded by consumers with the minimum environmental impact at all stages. This is a far reaching challenge as it involves a reformulation not only of production processes but of the products themselves. Whilst many consumers may be unwilling to reduce the overall levels of consumption to which they have become accustomed, they have proved willing to select the good which produces a reduced environmental impact. Companies need to focus their environmental strategies and subsequent green marketing campaigns on supplying goods with a sustainable differential advantage. In so doing the producer has to accept the responsibility for the environmental impact of the materials and processes used at the production stage and for the final product and its disposal. In many ways therefore, industry has to take on a whole range of new responsibilities towards the environment.

Sustainable development is not only about direct impact on the environment, however, and a corporate strategy dealing with narrow environmental performance measures is inadequate. We have suggested that a key part of the concept (which is often conveniently ignored by industry) is about equity. The massive inequality in wealth and standards of living displayed across the world makes sustainable development harder to achieve. Those living in the Third World often aspire to the standards of living of the First World and we know from an environmental stance such aspirations are presently not achievable. But what right does the First World have to deny other human beings development in the same unsustainable way in which they themselves have developed? Therefore we can see that environmental improvement is inextricably linked to wider issues of global concern which do need to be addressed. Equity has also to be tackled at the level of the firm, however. New forms of industrial organisation should seek to empower workers and increase their decision-making powers, to increase democracy in the workplace and to share profits with the workforce, alongside improving environmental performance. This demands a more holistic and ethical approach to doing business which values workers as an integral and valuable part of the organisation rather than a resource to be hired and fired as external market conditions change.

## THE CORPORATE RESPONSE TO SUSTAINABLE DEVELOPMENT

Companies are faced with the challenge of integrating environmental considerations into their production and marketing plans. There is always an incentive, however, for profit-maximising firms seeking short-term rewards, to opt out and become a free rider (assuming that everyone else will be environmentally conscious such that their own pollution will become negligible). However, environmental legislation in Western economies is increasingly plugging the gaps which allow this to happen and firms (and their directors) attempting to hide their illegal pollution are now subject to severe penalties. Even before then though, businesses should recognise that it is not only ethical to be environmentally friendly, but with the growth of consumer awareness in the environmental area, it will also be 'good business' in a more traditional sense.

Firms clearly have a role to play in the development of substitutes for non-renewable resources and innovations which reduce waste and use energy more efficiently. They also have a role in processing those materials in a way which brings about environmental improvements. For many products (e.g. cars and washing machines), the major area of environmental damage occurs in their usage. Firms often have the opportunity of reducing this damage at the design stage and when new products are being developed there is a whole new opportunity for considering both the use and disposal of the product.

Within the pluralist society in which we live a whole range of pressures are beginning to create the preconditions which are necessary to encourage businesses to respond to the environmental challenge. Industry is beginning to develop the new technologies and techniques which may help to move the global economy towards sustainability and whilst accepting that the answer will not lie in technology alone, we must continue to do so. The rapid growth of public environmental awareness in recent years has also placed new pressures on industry. These pressures can take many forms as individuals collectively exercise their environmental conscience as customers, employees, investors, voters, neighbours and responsible citizens.

Throughout the developed world the approach of governments has been to respond to increasing public concern for the environment by developing policy frameworks for environmental protection. Environmental policies and their associated legislation impose new costs and generate new opportunities for industry and change the competitive climate that faces industry. In the market place, survival and success is often linked to the ability of companies to be flexible and to respond to the new pressures put before them. As consumers become ever more sophisticated, these pressures are set to increase. But the consumer continues (rightly) to see industry as one of the major contributors to environmental degradation. For the ethical organisation the solution is simple. Rather than being seen as the cause of the environmental problem, industry must respond and show itself to be the solution to the problem. Once again though, that requires commitment to the idea of environmental improvement and a willingness to consider new forms of organisation which directly address the competing objectives of stakeholders with differing amounts of power.

Environmental strategy must therefore begin with real commitment on the part of the whole organisation. This may mean a change in corporate culture and management has an important role to play. In leading that commitment and laying out the organisation's corporate objectives with respect to the environment, management has to be the catalyst for change. Indeed it needs to rethink its whole rationale and reassess the very structures in its own organisation which act as impediments to change. Moreover, change has to be on-going and management must be ever mindful of the full range of (often competing) objectives to which it is subject. Management has to find compromise between these objectives if they conflict and design corporate strategies which are operational, consistent and achievable. Change will have to be addressed in a systemic way, dealing with the company as a whole rather than in a compartmentalised way. There is also a need to look towards the 'larger picture' rather than being driven by

11

product-specific considerations. Moreover, corporate structures should not be seen as rigid and the identification and development of corporate strengths seen as more important than the continuation of 'business as usual'. When it comes to the integration of environmental considerations, cooperative strategies need also to be considered. All too often competition has been the dominant ideology in business, but increasingly cooperative strategies between businesses and involving the public and regulatory agencies can bring about benefits which are environmentally sustainable. Single-minded competitive strategies run the risk of isolating businesses from new developments, expertise and public opinion which are invaluable to the environmentally aware company.

## SUSTAINABLE DEVELOPMENT, INTERNATIONAL TRADE AND THE GLOBAL ECONOMY

One of the characteristics of post-war Europe has been growing integration associated with European economic union. But that trend, more recently, has been mirrored in other parts of the world. International trade is dominated by the global triad of Europe, North America and Japan and all OECD countries have found their economies becoming more interdependent and interrelated through the growth of trade, technology transfer and global communications networks. Through the mass media it has often been models of Western consumer culture which have been relayed across the planet and into the Third World. Yet global inequality persists between the higher income and lower income countries and there are considerable differences within the lower income countries themselves.

In many ways, no country can see itself as independent. The global spread of industrial activity along with the expansion of information systems means that no country can insulate itself from its external economic climate. Neither can countries insulate themselves from the growing pollution flows caused by industrialisation and consumerism. Perhaps most intrusive, however, are the activities of the transnational corporations (TNCs) who bring with them their own corporate cultures, dominate international trade and production and are therefore to be held responsible for significant levels of transnational environmental damage. In the decade between 1980 and 1990 the Worldwatch Institute has estimated that gross world output of goods and services grew from

US$4.5 trillion to US$20 trillion, and international trade grew by approximately 4 per cent per year (Brown, 1991).

The rapid evolution of an international economic system has not been matched by international political integration or international laws to regulate that system. The consequence is that many transnational corporations operate above the law, above national boundaries and are able to set their own international economic agenda. Moreover, by creating a situation where many Third World countries are dependent on their patronage, employment and technology, they often wield considerable political power as well. This is hardly a scenario which can be reconciled with sustainable development.

Since the 1980s we have seen an increasing move towards the liberal market version of the capitalist economy. By the beginnings of the 1990s there were many former communist countries putting radical and austere policies in place to introduce a market mechanism into their economies and to privatise previously state-run companies. However, the process of reform has taken much longer than expected, has resulted in significant costs associated with human suffering and in some countries has resulted in a nationalist backlash. Foreign investment into Central and Eastern Europe has also been disappointing and is still blocked by political uncertainty, environmental degradation and infrastructural backwardness.

Third World governments have also been attracted towards the liberal free market model, seeing it as the system which is able to deliver the goods and raise general levels of material prosperity. Where the Third World has been wary of adopting laissez faire economic policies they have been encouraged along that path by institutions such as the World Bank and the IMF who link the provision of loans to conditions relating to structural adjustment. This has meant that financial support and advice has been linked to the implementation of market friendly structural reform in the economy in question.

Despite all the pains of transition, however, it is likely that the Third World and the former Eastern bloc will want to continue to move towards liberal capitalism, attracted by Western levels of prosperity and consumption. Whilst the time scales for achieving such targets are uncertain there seems little doubt that some countries will achieve greatly increased levels of national output and per capita income. But as Carley and Christie (1992) point out, ironically, the drive for economic growth and hunger for Western levels of consumption in the newly industrialising countries and the ex-Communist world are developing precisely at the point at which consumerism in the West is beginning to appear socially self-defeating and ecologically unsustainable.

The enormous expansion of world trade has been a characteristic of the spread of capitalism and fundamental to the internationalisation of the industrial system. The central institution which lays out the terms of engagement in the international trade system and which monitors trade centres around the General Agreement of Tariffs and Trade (GATT). The Uruguay Round of GATT negotiations on removing trade barriers began in 1986 and was completed in 1993. Environmental considerations were largely ignored during this process reflecting the sad fact that issues of international trade and environmental management are seen as separate and discrete. Indeed, whilst at the Rio Summit governments and other agencies made declarations in support of the principles of sustainable development; when involved in the GATT negotiations, they were making decisions which could undermine progress towards sustainability.

GATT has consistently acted in favour of free trade and against environmental protection. It has consistently linked environmental issues to the issue of protectionism and has ignored issues of sustainability. In 1991 the GATT overruled an American ban on imports of tuna fish from Mexico (claimed to be fished in such a way as to kill an unacceptable number of dolphins) on the grounds that such a restriction would violate free trade. Indeed, the GATT view is that restrictions on trade, claimed on environmental grounds, would be more likely to be mere excuses for protectionism, rather than real attempts to reduce environmental damage. One is tempted to ask whatever happened to the precautionary principle?

## THE CULTURE OF CONSUMERISM

It is all so easy to put the blame on industry for the bulk of environmental degradation and this book focuses on the strategies which we need to follow to significantly reduce that impact. But we must also examine the reverse side of the coin which is consumerism. Industry growth and consumerism are, of course, inextricably linked. Consumerism is the vehicle upon which industry can expand, but the promotion of goods by industry also fuels consumerism. At the global level the issues are also intertwined. The industrialised nations are well aware of the problems associated with ozone depletion, global warming and the loss of biodiversity. They know that the economic expansion and growth of the Third World threaten to make the situation worse, but they cannot deny other countries the right to improve living standards from often very low bases. It seems evident that the planet could not sustain the globalisation of a Western consumer lifestyle, but governments are less willing to accept that there must be a limit to material consumption.

One of the major factors which has allowed consumerism to boom has been the massive advances in technology and technological capability. This has allowed more raw materials to be extracted and more to be processed and distributed in less time with less labour. That technology has been concentrated in the West, of course. The result has been that the scale of Western consumption compared with that elsewhere is increasingly diverse. According to the United Nations (UNDP, 1992) the 1.25 billion people in the advanced industrialised countries consume vastly more, on all key indicators, than the 3.4 billion who are adequately fed and clothed and the billion or more who live in absolute poverty. The 5 per cent of the world's population who live in the USA consume around one-third of the world's resources.

Although we might argue that history can provide us with all sorts of evidence to suggest that consumerism is not particularly new, a characteristic which we must accept is that the sheer scale of consumption is of a different order to anything known in pre-industrial times or periods of modernity. Mass consumption and the legitimation of individualism (which translates into consumerist attitudes) rather than collectivity is a characteristic of modern society. Society has become increasingly competitive, and cooperative and collectivist attitudes at the level of the local community have been replaced by independent, insular living where money becomes the measure of success and status. Cultural forces are marginalised and notions of local (or even national) self-sufficiency replaced by a reliance on trade of world commodities produced by an international, industrialised market.

The dominant culture which has been created through the growth of consumerism is now transmitted globally through mass communications technology and networks. In particular, it is the power of advertising and the persuasiveness and pervasiveness of sophisticated marketing strategies which promotes a link between well-being, status and consumption. So-called green advertising has its roots in consumerism and has therefore done little to promote environmentalism. Most green advertising campaigns have therefore been cynical attempts to increase market share and profitability without any real regard to the principles of sustainability.

The power of the transnational corporations is further strengthened through the global images which they are able to present using mass communications technology including satellite networks and associated broadcasting opportunities. Thus the globalisation of the industrial system not only makes the transnational organisation more powerful but it replaces local culture with an imported, generic, Western-based alternative. Thus there is a gradual erosion of local cultural distinctiveness in production and consumption and a spread in the desire for the imported products most associated with Western affluence. Such cultural control is hardly compatible with local action, self-determinism and individual empowerment needed to move us towards a more sustainable model of economic activity.

There must nevertheless be limits to consumerism. Indeed these fall into two types. Firstly, there are the limits to growth imposed by the possible physical exhaustion of many of the world's key resources. But before we ever reach that situation it is more likely that we will see another limit to consumerism and the culture associated with materialistic consumption. This limit will be imposed by social and environmental change. Ecological imbalance, environmental degradation, the growth in the number of major environmental disasters and the breakdown of aspects of social order are all a function of overproduction, overconsumption and associated inequalities between the rich and the poor.

According to commentators such as Durning (1991) there is little correlation between high levels of consumption and personal happiness. Indeed, Hirsch (1977) argues that there is something fundamentally self-defeating in modern consumption patterns. He notes the widespread dissatisfaction that accompanies the pursuit of affluence. His argument is that individuals only get satisfaction out of affluence by owning 'positional goods' which remain scarce. But the growth in wealth and the increased availability of goods means that positional goods become, over time, less valued. Therefore the individual in pursuit of happiness via materialism is constantly disappointed and having continually to find and pay for the next new purchase. The debate surrounding whether or not consumption equates with happiness and satisfaction is, however, of far less importance compared with the issue of consumption and sustainability.

It has already been argued that there must be clear limits to consumption and a growth in consumerism must therefore be incompatible with sustainable development. The challenge is therefore to translate this fact into policies which are able to correct the situation. To date there has been very little thought about this process except by those neo-classical economists who see the answer as internalising the social and environmental costs of consumption into the prices paid for consuming goods. The emphasis has therefore been put on calculating the full costs of externalities such as environmental damage and including these in the prices paid by consumers. The 'polluter pays' principle which establishes the foundation of much environmental policy is an attempt to undertake such an exercise. There are nevertheless certain problems with that sort of approach. Firstly, it assumes that we can accurately assess these additional costs. But all such analyses are open to large margins of error and often come down to personal judgements about the value of an asset or artefact to an undefined population. Secondly, for the cost internalisation approach to be fully effective, compensation must be paid for the use, for example, of an environmental asset. This requires that property rights are clearly defined. But for so many environmental goods (e.g. the air and the deep seas) no such property rights exist. Thirdly, such a full cost accounting methodology relies on deciding what should be included as an important cost and therefore internalised, and what should be excluded and ignored. Whilst we might all agree that direct pollution from the production of a good should be internalised, what about issues which may be less direct such as the impact on indigenous populations of the Third World who mine raw materials, the animals which may be displaced from their natural habitats in such a process or the families of people who die in road accidents caused in part by an increase in freight traffic. The question relates to where the boundaries are established (which is a social, ethical and practical issue); the answer to which will differ widely according to basic perceptions of policy makers.

Perhaps then the use of the market mechanism, which is what the 'polluter pays' approach relies upon, is not sufficient in itself to control the negative effects of overconsumption. There is clearly a role for the political dimension to play, not only, however, at the national level, but also at local levels and international levels. But here there is inevitable conflict between the aims and objectives of local, national and international politicians. Moreover, there will be inevitable problems surrounding the nature of equity within the Western industrialised countries and between them and the rest of the world.

One of the first questions to be addressed revolves around how much is enough. Just what should be the limits of consumption and who is to determine these? Such questions inevitably lead to consideration of equity and equality. Within the Western economies there needs to be a debate over the distribution of income, wealth and opportunity. Between countries the same issue needs to be discussed in the context of much wider disparities. If there is to be a limit put on consumption then we must also ask how the available resources are to be distributed. To simply continue to allocate goods to those with the greatest number of monetary votes, however, would seem to put the whole system back in doubt.

We need therefore to think more holistically about the future shape of societies and the future organisation of the global economy. To impose change through political action via the market mechanism and legislation is only one part of the solution. To tackle overconsumption by tackling demand will be insufficient and there is a need to tackle supply as well. That means making businesses more aware of their activities and convincing them of the need for radical change in the way they carry out their businesses. The starting point must be to make the modern business enterprise challenge its very reason for being and to encourage, persuade, cajole or force businesses to take an ethical stance. When businesses come to realise that we operate in a no-win game and that if they carry on operating in simplistic ways in order to maximise profits, they will eventually destroy their own markets by destroying the fundamentals of the planet on which we survive, then perhaps they will begin again to question their very aims and objectives and return to some fundamental ethical questions. That will take time, but we do not have very much time. Businesses and their owners need to be convinced of the need to act in a proactive way and to strive together towards sustainable development. There is an urgent need for education programmes to convince companies of that need and to provide them with some of the tools to help them to move towards a sustainable future. This book attempts to make a small contribution to that educational process and to the necessary process of challenging accepted norms and procedures. There is a need for us all to be more creative and imaginative and not to be held back by notions of barriers imposed by 'the real world'. Whose world is it anyway and whose reality is it?

## THE MEANING OF 'GREENING'

The greening of industry is a term much talked about but rather less thought about. It lacks a clear definition, remains troublesomely ambiguous and although it has become a popular target for academic research it is underdeveloped in terms of theory and untested along empirical lines. Authors such as Gladwin (1993) argue that for research on industrial greening to be broadly utilisable then there is a need to take a more scientific approach to it. This would involve an adequate description and classification of greening, the generalisability of findings and the predictability of conclusions. But is this not simply asking too much? In the postmodern world we must ask whether such meaning does and can exist. We must consider whether it can ever, any more, be possible to generalise from specific observations and in terms of greening we must ask whether is it a single process capable of classification at all. If we are to discuss the meaning of greening then it is not possible to accurately describe and predict. A more useful exercise therefore would seem to be to prescribe and define what greening ought to be. Central to this process we must consider where the concept of greening fits into our ultimate aim of sustainable development.

Let us begin however with an overview of what greening seems to mean at the moment, from a number of different perspectives on change. Figure 1.1 provides a crude 'spectrum of greening' which measures change. At one end is superficial change and at the other is fundamental change. Ten different forms of environmental strategy are chosen to reflect stages in the greening of industry along a ten-point scale. These strategies are categorised by the basic ideology underpinning them, beginning with a simple reactive ideology and ending with an acceptance of the need to base a new ideology around creativity.

Low down on the spectrum of greening are those firms for whom the greening process is fundamentally about add-on pollution control. Those firms are motivated merely by the need for

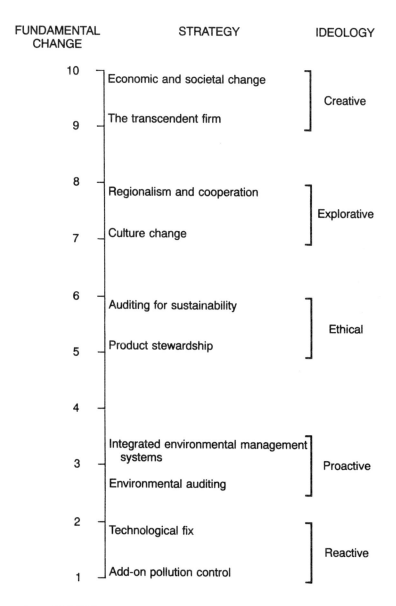

*Figure 1.1* The spectrum of greening

compliance and see pollution prevention as a necessity which adds to their costs. Such firms and such thinking is not unusual. To many, greening is to be found in the practical, technology-based action which, whilst often proactive, sees change in stark 'technological fix' terms. For example, a rethinking of processes through design for disassembly, rethinking traditional notions of disposability, toxic reduction through clean technology and an emphasis on energy and waste management are common amongst such firms. Essentially however these are reactive strategies.

More proactive firms are beginning to see a role for assessing, monitoring and acting on their environmental impacts through an environmental auditing methodology. The process of auditing is simply an information gathering exercise and it requires a commitment to a cycle of improvement at the very least. Those firms benefitting most from the auditing exercise will be those who have introduced integrated environmental management systems which represent a step towards a more holistic view of business strategy. Environmental auditing and environmental management systems approaches are dealt with in detail in chapter 3.

Those companies which see greening as an activity which goes beyond the processes which take place on an particular site or within the organisation more widely are increasingly committing themselves to product stewardship strategies. Thus they take responsibility for the products they produce from cradle to grave (see chapter 5). In other words they undertake a full life cycle assessment of their environmental impacts from the extraction of raw materials, through distribution and processing, to sale, use and disposal. Companies embarking on strategies involving the concept of auditing for sustainability (see chapter 4) examine the impact of all their products and activities in terms of wider definitions of environmental management which move us towards sustainability. Thus they not only measure direct environmental impacts but wider social impacts on, for example, ecosystems, animals and indigenous populations in the Third World. This leads us towards much more ethical ways of doing business.

Ultimately sustainability requires us to change the way we do business. This requires us to think about the very way in which we organise the workplace, the way we treat and respond to workers' needs and the very relationship between the business and the rest of society. The process of greening here must be explorative at two levels. Firstly, we must look towards culture change within the organisation to change its behaviour, objectives and outlook (this is discussed in chapter 6). Secondly, we must increasingly recognise the benefits of acting cooperatively rather than competitively in managing environmental improvement and defining sustainable strategies which are effective and accepted at a local level. Thus more fundamental change will alter the internal dimensions of the firm and change its relationship with the world around it through policies based on regional development. The radical change here is a move away from the nationally or transnationally based organisation towards regional suppliers facilitating local purchasing policies and a degree of regional independence.

The most fundamental forms of greening have not really been considered in any detail yet except by deep green ecologists who are still seen as being on the fringes of the environmental discourse. However, new ideas revolving around radical change require us to be more creative in our thinking. Ultimately, the challenge of sustainable development will require some degree of economic and societal change. Many keen on the regional approach to greening argue that the bioregional model offers the most sustainable future (see chapter 8). Within such a model firms as we know them may cease to exist. Where firms do exist, then to be compatible with sustainability in the longer term, they must transcend all other demands, priorities, norms and objectives and place sustainability as their number one priority. No firm is close to that, but it is time to begin thinking about how that may be possible and what that organisation may look like.

We must of course remember that whatever the extent of greening it is a necessary but not a sufficient condition for sustainable development. In tandem with the greening of industry, this chapter has pointed towards other areas where action is required. Poverty alleviation, population control, health crises, regional conflicts, inequality, famine and starvation, consumerism, political structures, the power of transnational corporations and a multitude of other issues all need to be tackled. This book begins to tackle only one part of the problem – the relationship between sustainable development and the business world. It is hoped that it can nevertheless make a small contribution to the enormous task of moving towards a sustainable future. To do that, however, business strategy must be seen in the context of societal change.

## THE SOCIETAL DIMENSION

In any discussion about the environmentally aware enterprise or in relation to the tools of corporate environmental management the concept of sustainable development is at the forefront. We have argued however that that term is being used by corporate environmentalists to justify an incremental approach to improvement stressing the environment as a single-issue subject and leaving aside the key and equally important concepts of equity and futurity. Sustainable development is a radical concept and as such it must be removed from such predictable patterns of interpretation. It is not a concept which lends itself to the piecemeal marginalism which we have seen to date and as a radical concept it demands more imaginative and creative vehicles to put it into practice. In its radical form (Engel and Engel, 1990), sustainabilty combines independent development with the concept of bioregionalism discussed later in this book.

One of the challenges of sustainable development is for us to consider modes of industrial organisation as well as the internal organisation of the firm which will lead us towards a future which promotes environmental protection and equity. If one starts with the premise that the present structure of capitalism has contributed significantly to environmental degradation and increases inequity and inequality then our challenge is either to point towards new modes of organisation within a post-capitalist structure or to abandon capitalism altogether.

Until recently it was the concept and trends inherent in modernism which defined many of the organisational aspects of both the economy and society as a whole and individual firms within them. Modernism involved a continuous process of redefining and reshaping of what went before, in pursuit of general principles that were thought to have been desirable for the universal human good (Pepper, 1993). Thus small scale production was replaced by mass production facilitated through mass communications and thus devaluing individuality. Taylorist principles were introduced into the organisation treating workers as simple neoclassical factors of production and managed by rigid hierarchies. Modernism saw the justification for increased materialism, increased (over)consumption, saturated mass consciousness based on manufactured images, notions of instantaneity, temporariness and disposability. Perhaps even more importantly, it was the vehicle for the introduction of dualist thinking. Such dualism has led to a tendency to separate society and nature, i.e. to see them as separate and opposite.

It is the assertion of this chapter that contemporary writings on environmental management within organisations (most typically business organisations) are based on over-simple, independent categorisations which, in turn, hide the complexities of the environmental debate and the complexities of the individual business organisation. Postmodern analysis, on the other hand, requires us to distance ourselves from assumptions of unity and therefore to question the generic codes of conduct which make up contemporary corporate environmental philosophy (see chapter 2). It is argued therefore that there is no single ideology of universal relevance and culture becomes divided into discrete spheres. This being the case, we are forced to challenge simple categorisations, structures and codes which purport to move us towards sustainability. Nevertheless, it is argued that within the postmodern context the trend of post-Fordist production allows us to revisit concepts such as bioregionalism within a contemporary setting.

According to commentators such as Power (1990) postmodernism stands for the 'death of reason' and therefore offers a frontal assault on methodological unity (Hassard and Parker, 1993). It gives validity to all views and perspectives. Through the postmodern method of 'deconstruction' (Derrida, 1978) a whole range of philosophical pillars are brought down. The ambiguity inherent in postmodernism offsets the tendency of commentators to make simple categorisations. Harvey (1989) argues that postmodernism rediscovers the vernacular in architecture, emphasises the discontinuity in history, the indeterminacy in science and the dignity of all possible perspectives in ethics, politics and culture.

There is therefore a need to move away from the simplistic view of society implicit in corporate environmental strategies, and postmodernism provides us with an approach which describes the 'world out there' more accurately. The 'post' prefix is related to a number of concepts which reflect specific features of a postmodern society. One of the most important of these is the notion of post-Fordism (Piore and Sabel, 1984) which characterises the business organisation in a flexible and dynamic way. A theme associated with the 'post' prefix is that the social and economic structures reproduced since the industrial revolution are now fragmenting into diverse networks often held together by information technology, flexibility and new modes of organisation. Hall and Jacques (1989) imply in their work on 'New Times' that if we can understand these trends then we should be able to control them. But we should note that this understanding is fundamentally different to the neo-classical economic approach which sees organisations as acting and responding in rational economic ways capable of modelling and generalisation.

What postmodernism also exposes is the nature of empiricism. No matter how scientific it is, the empirical process can never produce an accurate correspondence with reality. Instead, it commonly produces a process of professional self-justification. So-called independent research is limited by the discourses which are already shared within a particular scientific community. The evidence which is produced is, in turn, interpreted and justified within a restricted linguistic domain. As an empirical process starts with its theoretical assumptions intact, data produced through experimentation are defined by reference to an existing theoretical spectrum (Gergen, 1992). Findings produced through empirical science therefore do little more than reflect pre-existing intellectual categories.

If one accepts a postmodernist approach there is a seeming impasse in dealing with environmental issues at the firm level. Indeed, even the notion of sustainable development might be challenged for focusing on a particular model which exists within a well-defined theoretical paradigm. However, perhaps with some prestidigitation, we ought not to see sustainable development as an end and as an aim but as a mode of action which, in turn, has to be addressed in different ways by organisations operating with differing objectives and cultures. Postmodernism therefore indicates that simple procedures often embedded in codes of conduct and generic models of environmental improvement at the firm level may be inappropriate.

## CONCLUSIONS

According to Steward (1989) the growing green picture is intertwined with a renewal of collectivism, universalism and social purpose. Interdependence and sustainability set the terms for individual and social choice and green politics represents a pattern of change in which collective identity and universal values assume a new status and significance. The analysis of the new needs to embrace the dynamic of these relationships and not see any one ideology, cultural form or mode of action as dominant over others. Neither can moral aspirations and direct challenges to current systems and structures (which form the bedrock of capitalism) be consigned to the dustbin of 'naive, unworkable radicalism'. We need to be imaginative and creative. We need to be forward looking and accept that present economic and political structures act as a barrier to any improvement which will deliver sustainable development.

The way forward seems to be to combine the collective and the individual, to empower people towards a common purpose with personal choice and to develop the organisation so that it strives towards new imperatives while developing the individual and individuality. This approach stresses the need for new social contracts, for new relationships between owners, managers and workers and the revisitation of notions of industrial democracy, participation, cooperation and collectivism. The assuetudes developed in the 1980s have moved us away from these important notions which have been replaced by the apothegms of individualism.

Of course, environmental concerns challenge established political forms. Sustainable development demands a global approach (based on local action and organisation), it demands a reconsideration of equity and a new stress on equality. There are serious limits to the capacity of national sovereignty to deal with the threats to the environment. There may be a need for new national and supranational forums and a recognition of interdependence at the global level (although real action should be at the local or regional level). Moreover, such institutions need also to be more creative and leave aside accepted wisdom and theories which maintain the status quo. The growth of uncertainty and conflict between the 'experts' as to the severity of environmental risk has led to a recognition of the limits of rationality alone and an enhanced status for explicit values (Steward, 1989). Existing structures premised on professional exclusiveness and expert consensus do little but maintain the power of the dominant ideologies. We need to further develop the notions of individual responsibility and collective strategy at the political level and drive this down to the organisational level. The new culture needs to be eclectic and cooperative, individualist and collective.

Green thinking draws on a clear moral stance. It provides a radical challenge which is in our grasp if we are willing to challenge power and reconstruct economic structures in a sustainable way. At the heart of that reconstruction is the need to define and develop new flexible ways of carrying out industrial activity. One of the core values of the green movement is the emphasis on qualitative as opposed to quantitative objectives as a measure of social process. And this is where the political is synonymous with the personal. Schumacher (1974) reflects the views of many in asserting that when it comes to action we need small units because action is a highly personal affair.

The rest of this book therefore explores in more detail the sorts of business-related strategies which firms will need to adopt firstly to meet the needs of the environmental challenge and secondly to be compatible with sustainable development. At the very least the whole approach must be based on a sound ethical ideology. Within that context we need to explore contemporary environmental management tools and improve their implementation through a more demanding methodology and a widening of the definition of the environment. We need to explore the role of culture change within the organisation. Moreover ultimately we need to look towards new modes of industrial organisation which (unlike present ones) will be compatible with sustainability. Because this is a book about sustainable development it is a book about the future. Not everything discussed in the book is achievable in the short term but it is important that we begin the debate now!

# 2

# BUSINESS ETHICS AND CORPORATE ENVIRONMENTAL PERFORMANCE

## INTRODUCTION

The starting point in this chapter is to argue that corporate environmental issues are a subset of business ethics and that by considering the structures and procedures which define the ethics of a company we ought be able to say something about the prospects and pre-conditions for corporate environmental improvement. However, the systematic treatment of business ethics has been neglected in most advanced economies. Within the social sciences we have seen the study of political economy, for example, replaced by economic science and positive economics and this has placed an emphasis on theories of optimisation rather than sustainability at the firm level. To begin to tackle the challenges which the environment provides us with we must begin to redress this balance. Western economies have developed along particular paths with an emphasis on industrial growth, efficiency (defined in narrow monetary terms) and performance (usually defined by profits and increases in share prices). The politics associated with Thatcherism and Reaganism led to the common cry that 'there is no alternative' and the development of a narrow, profit-centred corporate ethic.

There are those who suggest, however, that social responsibility and environmental considerations can no longer be ignored in the context of an ethical (and indeed efficient) approach to doing business. Hartley (1993), for example, suggests that the interests of a firm are actually best served by scrupulous attention to the public interest and by seeking a trusting relationship with the various stakeholders with which a firm is involved. In the process, society is also best served because the firm is forced to consider a whole range of competing objectives and to move away from activities which are derived from short term performance indicators. These various stakeholders which the firm must consider are its customers, suppliers, employees, shareholders, the financial institutions, local communities and government. The stakeholder concept stresses the idea that a company has responsibilities to all these groups (even though they will have unequal amounts of power) and will be involved in balancing the often competing demands put upon it. A company's ethical stance will therefore be influenced both by internal values and by pressures exerted on it from external sources.

## BUSINESS ETHICS

The starting point must therefore be to provide some sort of definition of business ethics. This is difficult because it will depend on both the values of individuals working in the organisation and particularly on the culture created by the individual ethics of senior management, and on any codes of conduct which formally exist within the organisation or standards adopted from external agencies. We do not observe one single ethical code in all parts of society, but different codes in different places and at different times and this is replicated within any business. We can, however, distinguish between 'personal value systems' which individuals will bring to the workplace and a 'formal business code' which may exist in some businesses through an explicit set of rules (Burke *et al.*, 1993). Perhaps more importantly, however, we ought to think about the 'actual value system' which is the moral climate experienced by staff in their daily business lives and will determine the behaviour of the firm as a whole, and a 'necessary value system', which is the minimum level of ethics (often equated with legal requirements) which has to exist for the firm to survive.

In a pluralistic society, social, cultural and organisational power structures will tend to interact with these value systems. Such interaction may bring about a consensus or norm in certain areas of business activity, but it may also result in conflict where the ultimate outcome will depend crucially on the balance of power. One of the phenomena we have seen in the last few years is a shift of some of that power towards the consumer and the general public and this has renewed the interest in business ethics and corporate responsibility.

Another issue which causes problems for those advocating stronger codes of business ethics is that not all desirable ethics are mutually consistent. In those circumstances, judgements have to be made based on valuing different ethical actions. This too is a significant source of conflict. Again though, outcomes will be determined by power structures and dominant ideologies will tend to arise. Such ideologies are nevertheless often a product of compromise and may not necessarily be first best solutions. This is particularly apparent when we compare the conduct of those companies who are implementing environmental management strategies, with the imperatives called for by the concept of sustainable development (Welford, 1993).

The study of business ethics is not new. In the nineteenth century, Utilitarian reformers highlighted the need for ethical principles to be part of the free enterprise system. Currently, the literature on business ethics and on ethics generally is vital and growing. A key issue, however, is that there are many dilemmas where major principles, held to be moral imperatives, can, in some circumstances, be incompatible. There must therefore exist some sort of hierarchy which places more emphasis on one principle than another. What we are clearly observing nowadays is the movement of environmental considerations up that hierarchy.

Ultimately, however, it is organisation which dictates the hierarchy of different principles. The various levels of organisation, from whole economic and political systems via institutions and organisations to individual relationships suggest particular hierarchies of principles (Donaldson, 1989). These hierarchies obviously shift over time and between different economic and political systems. They can be influenced, although that, in turn, will depend on power relationships. Many principles of business ethics might be considered somewhat abstract. A key issue therefore is how commonly accepted principles (such as improved environmental performance at the firm level) can be translated into practice. This has to be done via codes (legal and self-regulating), education, communication and information. But these vehicles for change are themselves open to manipulation by those with power and the best principles are not always translated into best practice. Increasingly, for example, people are agreeing with the principle of sustainable development, but the vehicles translating that into business practice have stopped far short of real sustainable solutions.

Because language is the basis of communication, it plays a crucial part in the translation of a principle into practice. Commonly, one person's technical term is another person's jargon. Again, the whole concept of sustainable development has come to mean a number of different things to different people. Terms such as sustainability, sustainable growth, sustained growth, sustainable development and sustaining organisations have become confused. Commonly they are associated with environmentalism and the key concepts of equity and futurity are sidelined. Moreover, when ethical outcomes are discussed, words such as moral, ethical, good, efficient, rational, effective, fair, best and improved, all come to mean different things in different circumstances. The meanings, connotations and overtones of words and phrases are often deployed in the conflicts and struggles for supremacy. The language of management is rich in emotive and ideological content and therefore what companies and managers say they are doing must be treated with healthy scepticism. What they are actually doing assessed against clearly defined principles and measures is much more important (see chapter 3). Hence in communicating their message about environmental performance companies must be open and honest and not be tempted along the road of self-gratification and over-statement which we so often observe.

According to Donaldson (1989) there has been a relative neglect of the systematic handling of values in business which has been self-conscious. The consequences of the neglect can be seen both in anxiety about industrial performance in the West and a rise of concern about moral or ethical issues. A patchy awareness of the problem is to be seen in the sporadic (and at times piecemeal) nature of attempts by governments to regulate industry. This is well illustrated by the uneven growth in environmental legislation in the West and the continued growth of ad hoc codes of conduct in this area.

All organisations operate an ethical code, whether they know it or not. This may not be at all times consistent but it is based on codes of conduct embedded into company culture and through the actions and decisions of senior management. Those codes will also be influenced by society's norms and in the business world by institutions and practices which stress the need to create wealth measured in quantitative financial terms. For any business which wishes to survive or avoid hostile takeover, the system necessarily pushes profits to the top of the corporate agenda and pushes other issues, such as environmental protection, down the agenda.

Moreover, there is no business practice, action or statement that cannot have an ethical dimension. Businesses serve a variety of purposes for different stakeholders. Therefore we might argue that as a necessary condition, business activities are justifiable only in so far as they can be shown to meet the legitimate requirements of stakeholders. However, these requirements can be and often are in conflict and can change over time. In identifying requirements and reconciling them we have major problems. Moreover, we have suggested that the principles, ideals and moral values upon which stakeholders' requirements are based can be in themselves contradictory. The traditional way of resolving these issues is for the firm to assume primacy over individuals, allowing it to pursue objectives dictated by senior management subject to financial constraints imposed by owners and lenders. Thus firms often adopt their own identity and culture and often exist outside the democratic framework. But we must realise that business ought to be a means and not an end, and it is a means for satisfying the requirements of all who have a legitimate claim.

It might be argued that any philosophy or course of action that doesn't take the public interest into consideration is intolerable in today's society (Hartley, 1993). Today's firms face more critical scrutiny from stakeholders and operate in a setting which is becoming more regulatory and litigious. The notion of public trust is also becoming more important. A clear measure of how far we have come towards a more responsive and responsible business climate is indicated by the fact that if a firm violates public trust then it is likely to be surpassed by its competitors, who will be eager to please customers by addressing their wants more accurately. Moreover, whilst the overwhelming majority of business dealings are non-controversial, any abuses increasingly receive considerable publicity, harming the image of business.

In order to remain economically active, firms need to learn from their mistakes or from those of other firms. They need to take care to avoid situations and actions that might harm their relationship with their various stakeholders. In the worst of all cases, where a firm faces a catastrophe, suddenly and without warning, its whole market image and business strategy can be destroyed. Examples of such events are increasingly commonplace. For example, in the case of Union Carbide, when one of its chemical plants in Bhopal, India leaked 40 tons of toxic chemicals, the event had (and still has) a profound effect on the reputation of that company. Although the company quickly rushed aid to the victims, it was bitterly condemned for complacency and the loose controls that permitted the accident to happen in the first place.

Environmental considerations are only one of many issues which might be included under the umbrella of business ethics. It is nevertheless an issue which has grown in importance. As a result of the many accidents and growing environmental damage caused by firms there have been increasing demands from consumers for firms to operate more ethically in this area. The consumer movement has fundamentally shaped and contributed to the significant increase in legislation and regulation at all levels of government. This has been aimed at preventing abuses in the marketplace and in the environment and therefore environmental management strategies are increasingly commonplace in the leading companies around the world. To date, however, environmental considerations have not been given enough attention within the framework of business ethics because dominant ideologies are being shaped more by short term financial considerations than by the need to do business in a sustainable way.

## CODES OF CONDUCT AND STANDARDS

Although there has been an increasing amount of regulation covering a range of environmental issues, the European Union's intent within its Fifth Environmental Action Plan has been to put more and more emphasis on market-based and voluntary measures. Coupled with this, deregulation measures, introduced by more right-wing governments to appease industry in some European countries, have meant even more emphasis being put on voluntary codes of conduct and standards. Of course, it was industry itself which lobbied for the European eco-management and audit scheme to be voluntary when the first draft suggested that it might be mandatory for the worst polluting industries. The design and definition of voluntary codes and standards are therefore important to consider.

Codes of conduct defined within an organisation or imported from elsewhere in the form of standards are usually associated with practical sets of rules and guidelines. They tend to be expressions of mixtures of technical, prudential and moral imperatives. They influence behaviour and therefore ethical outcomes. However, standards which are externally driven are typically expressed in a form that is well protected from discussion, expressing aims in a matter-of-fact language (Donaldson, 1989). In turn, therefore, a standard carries with it a dominant ideology which, because it is standardised, has a multiplier effect and increasing weight if the standard becomes a norm.

The adoption of codes of conduct and standards within any organisation necessarily raises a number of questions. The most obvious one concerns the type of sub-culture which a standard brings with it. Does it represent a piecemeal attempt to placate demands from pressure groups and consumers or is it a more serious attempt at ethical behaviour, for example? We ought also to ask how effective the codes are in promoting what they stand for? Taken together these questions provide a measure of the extent to which the standards are genuine and operational, rather than cynical and self-deluding.

Codes of conduct and particularly standards, which become accepted across firms in an industry or even across industries, are very powerful and we often see them written into contracts between organisations. We might be inclined to think that a standard promoting some sort of environmental improvement is a huge step forward and that companies who follow others in adopting such standards should be congratulated. But rather more analysis of the content and purpose of such a standard is necessary before we can reach an answer to that question. Without suggesting that environmental standards are indeed bad we must nevertheless consider whether, in fact, some standards push employees and customers into a set of values which verge on indoctrination. Stakeholders in those sorts of situations come to possess what Marxists see as false consciousness. In addition the fact that a standard is widely accepted does not guarantee that the values within it are not restricted or inconsistent. Values contained in standards can also be restricted when, for example (and typically), they exclude any consideration of the impact of a company's activities on indigenous populations in the Third World.

There is very little research on the generation, operation, monitoring and amendment of codes and standards. However, it is argued forcefully by Donaldson (1989) that because codes tend to be expressions of mixtures of technical, prudential and moral imperatives, and because they tend to vary in the extent to which they are or can be enforced, they cannot be regarded as the major vehicles for identifying and encouraging the practices which will raise the level of values in business and industry. Moreover, codes and standards are defined outside the normal democratic framework which determines laws. They are constructed by agencies (often professional bodies or representatives of senior management in industry) with their own motivations, values and interests. On this subject Donaldson and Waller (1980) point to a statement of Bernard Shaw when he asserted that professions can be conspiracies against the laity, and their codes, it may be added, are widely held to be primarily aimed at the protection of the members of the profession, rather than the public. Much the same accusation might be levelled against industry standards. Moreover, the matter of the development of codes and standards is bound up with the matter of enforcement. Codes which are not enforced or fail to deliver their expected outcomes for whatever reason might be thought of as little more than cynical expressions of pious hopes.

Much of what has been discussed here can be illustrated by reference to the Responsible Care Programme, which in itself provides a standard for firms operating in the chemicals industry to adopt. The Responsible Care Programme might be seen as one of the earliest environmental management systems standards used across companies. It is a voluntary code where performance is measured in terms of continuous improvement. Responsible Care is unique to the chemical industry and originated in Canada in 1984. Launched in 1989 in the UK by the Chemical Industries Association (CIA) the cornerstone of the system is commitment. Chief Executives of member companies are invited to sign a set of guiding principles pledging their company to make health, safety and environmental performance an integral part of overall business policy. Adherence to the principles and objectives of Responsible Care is a condition of membership of the Chemical Industries Association. All employees and company contractors have to be made aware of these principles. The guiding principles also require companies to:

- conform to statutory regulations;
- operate to the best practices of the industry;
- assess the actual and potential health, safety and environmental impacts of their activities and products;

- work closely with the authorities and the community in achieving the required levels of performance;
- be open about activities and give relevant information to interested parties.

A company operating the Responsible Care Programme is required to have a clear company policy and the communication of this is seen as vital. The key principle being used in the Responsible Care Programme is self-assessment. However, the CIA does assess the effectiveness of the programme across all firms by collecting indicators of performance from the firms. Companies are encouraged to submit six classes of data to the Association. Individual company data are not published but a national aggregate figure is published annually. This shows industry trends and enables individual companies to assess their own placing accordingly. The six indicators of performance are:

1 Environmental protection spending;
2 Safety and health (lost time, accidents for employees and contractors);
3 Waste and emissions:
   a discharges of 'red list' substances;
   b waste disposal;
   c an environmental index of five key discharges by site;
4 Distribution (all incidents);
5 Energy consumption (total on-site);
6 All complaints.

A key element of the Responsible Care system is the sharing of information and participation of employees and the local community. Local Responsible Care 'cells' operate for the exchange of information and experience between firms. Employee involvement is also encouraged and the CIA has established training programmes which set targets for appraisal. Firms are also encouraged to have community liaison groups and initiatives recognising the continuing need to forge improved relationships with the public.

However, in its three-year report of the Responsible Care programme (ENDS, 1993c) the CIA was implicitly forced to admit that the Responsible Care programme was not functioning in accordance with its aims. The main reason for this is that sites claiming to adhere to the Responsible Care standard were simply not adhering to its principles. Over the three-year reporting period only 57 per cent of firms made returns for all three years and only 74 per cent made any returns at all. Even more importantly, the third indicator of performance deals with waste and emissions where firms are supposed to report and environmental index by site designed to give a composite picture of gaseous, liquid and solid releases. Only one-third of the total firms supposed to be operating Responsible Care reported this data in full, and of those who reported the index, over 30 per cent reported a worsening environmental impact.

Codes of conduct are therefore nothing if they are not adhered to, and voluntary approaches often slip down a list of priorities when other pressing issues arise. It is perhaps not surprising that the lack of response from the chemical industry over Responsible Care occurred during a particularly bad economic recession. However, at the core of any strategy for environmental improvement has to be commitment and no standard or code of conduct can survive without that commitment. Whilst some chemical companies are clearly committed to improving their environmental performance it seems that too many are not adhering to the spirit of Responsible Care. Indeed, whilst some make efforts to follow the guidelines of the programme many more treat Responsible Care as a smoke screen. Many of those managers in the chemical industry who appear confident of their procedures to improve environmental performance are certainly either suffering from the false consciousness which was suggested earlier or are making much more cynical attempts to hide their environmental impact in an attempt to hang on to market share and profitability.

## THE CONTRIBUTION OF ETHICS TO ENVIRONMENTAL MANAGEMENT STRATEGIES

Ethics refers to standards of right conduct. Unfortunately, there is often not complete agreement as to what constitutes ethical behaviour. In the case of illegal and exploitative activities, there is not much dispute. But many practices fall into a grey area, where opinions may differ as to what is ethical and what is unethical and unacceptable. One possible example of environmental strategies which fall into that grey area relates to the eco-labelling of products and claims associated with the environmental friendliness of a product. These are examples of firms using tactics to persuade people to buy, often misleading customers into thinking they are getting a product which will not harm the environment, and exaggerating advertising claims. Unfortunately, some business firms have decided to 'walk on the edge' of ethical practices (Hartley, 1993). This is a dangerous strategy because the dividing line will be different for everybody. Moreover, what society once tolerated as acceptable behaviour is rapidly becoming unacceptable and firms which choose to position themselves so close to criticism will end up battling with time. To a large extent business ethics are firmly on the agenda in the 1990s. Society expects, and is now demanding, much more ethical conduct, whereas it had previously regarded questionable practices with apathy or ignorance.

It is now no longer justifiable to see business ethics as directly connected with the law and 'necessary value systems' are inappropriate. The relationship between ethical conduct and the law is sometimes confusing. Naive businesses might rationalise that actions within the law are therefore ethical and perfectly justifiable. But an 'if it's legal, it's ethical' attitude disregards the fact that the law codifies only that part of ethics which society feels so strongly about that it is willing to support it with physical force (Westing, 1968).

Many businesses assume that the more strictly one interprets ethical behaviour, the more profits suffer. Certainly, the muted sales efforts that may result from toning down product claims or refusing to buy raw materials which result in the exploitation of indigenous populations may hurt profits. Yet a strong argument can also be made that scrupulously honest and ethical behaviour is better for business and for profits. Well-satisfied customers tend to bring repeat business and it is therefore desirable to develop trusting relationships with not only customers but also personnel, suppliers, and the other stakeholders with which a firm deals. An unbending disavowal of the unethical practices such as false environmental claims and improper waste management can, in turn, create a healthier business culture for an entire industry. A firm's reputation for honest dealings and environmental action can also be a powerful competitive advantage. Ethical conduct is not incompatible with profitability but it does change timescales. It is more compatible with maximising profits in the long run, even though in the shorter term disregard of these ethical principles may yield more profits.

Unfortunately, the perception that unethical and shady practices will yield more sales and profits still prevails in many organisations. Given the institutional setting of the modern capitalist economy there are certain factors which can be identified that tend to motivate those less than desirable practices. These include an overemphasis on short term performance, the dominance of competition over cooperation, expediency and indifference, and a dominant ideology towards environmental management which stresses piecemeal approaches rather than a strategy based on the principles of sustainable development. Let us examine these issues in a little more detail.

## The overemphasis on short term performance

In most firms, career development and higher salaries depend on achieving greater sales and profits. This is true not only for individual employees and executives but for departments, divisions, and the entire firm. The value that stockholders and investors, creditors, and suppliers place on a firm depends to a large extent on growth. In turn, the dominant measure of growth is increasing sales and profits. The better the growth rate, the more money available for further expansion by investors and creditors at attractive rates. Suppliers and customers are more eager to do business. Top-quality personnel and executives are also more easily attracted.

In particular, the dominant drive would seem to be towards profits and profit maximisation. This is justified by economists such as Friedman (1963) who argues that 'few trends could so thoroughly undermine the very foundations of our free society as the acceptance by corporate officials of social responsibility other than to make as much money for their stockholders as possible' (p. 133). Friedman's view and that of many others simply neglects the responsibility that all actors in society have to benefit society in terms which are wider than the narrowly based performance measures which he adopts.

The emphasis on quantitative measures of performance and on growth, in particular, has some potential negative consequences. In particular, it tends to push environmental issues down the corporate agenda. If growth can be achieved at the expense of marginal environmental damage then little account will be taken of the real impact of this damage. The emphasis on growth becomes all pervading and environmental objectives (which may or may not exist) are compromised. Even where the objective is to maximise growth subject to other constraints, growth can easily be justified by devaluing the importance of those other constraints. Moreover, with a dominant growth strategy, people are not measured on the basis of their moral contribution to the business enterprise. Hence they become caught up in a system which is characterised by an ethic foreign to and often lower than the ethics of human beings (Holloway and Hancock, 1968). That tends to devalue the role of the worker and of those involved further down the supply chain. It is little wonder therefore, when it comes to the consideration of the effect that the production and processing of raw materials might have on indigenous Third World populations, that very little weight is attached to the needs and aspirations of these peoples.

## The dominance of competition over cooperation

An intensely competitive environment, especially if coupled with a firm's inability to differentiate products substantially or to cement segments of the market, will tend to motivate unethical behaviour (Hartley, 1993). The actions of one or a few firms in a fiercely competitive industry may generate a follow-the-leader situation, requiring the more ethical competitors to choose lower profits or lower ethics. Moreover, in a fiercely competitive environment the objective of the firm is dominated by the need to increase market share, to stay one step ahead of competitors and therefore to adopt isolationist and independent strategies. To succeed in the marketplace businesses feel the need to cut costs, to downgrade other objectives, which might be perceived as expensive, and to cut corners where possible.

That is not to suggest that competition is bad but that its dominance does militate against the opportunities which can be brought about through cooperation. Moreover, environmental issues are often overlooked because they are perceived as adding to costs with any benefits being somewhat intangible. Cooperative strategies can lead to synergetic benefits to businesses within a region or industry and can prevent the wasteful duplication of resources in many areas (Welford, 1993). Such a strategy leads to the sharing of experiences and the sharing of the costs and benefits of research and development which, in turn, encourages all firms to adopt best practices and procedures.

## Expediency and indifference

The attitude of expediency and indifference to the customers' best interests accounts for both complacency and unethical practices. These attitudes, whether permeating an entire firm or affecting only a few individuals, are hardly conducive to repeat business and customer loyalty. They are more prevalent in firms with many small customers and in those firms where repeat business is relatively unimportant. But such attitudes also have an impact on environmental issues. They tend to mean that corners are cut and due care is not taken to protect the environment. They tend to increase the unnecessary use of resources and generate excessive waste and they tend to militate against the adoption of systems and procedures which can prevent accidents and environmental damage. Moreover, indifference and apathy tend to militate against accepting the responsibility which every individual and every firm has in protecting the environment now and into the future.

## The dominant ideology towards environmental management

Significant evidence exists that management trends which become popular exert a strong influence on the on-going techniques of corporate management. New concepts which are successfully implemented in certain organisations become accepted, become dominant and even when they are inappropriate become the norm (Mintzberg, 1979). DiMaggio and Powell (1983) offer three explanations for this phenomenon. Firstly, organisations will submit to both formal and informal pressures from other organisations upon which they depend. Secondly, when faced with uncertainty organisations may model themselves on organisations that have seemed to be successful and adopt the sorts of techniques which they see being introduced. Thirdly, normative pressures which stem from a degree of professionalism amongst management can cause the adoption of 'fashionable' management techniques. Universities, training institutions, standard-setters and professional associations are all vehicles for the development of these normative rules.

These are precisely the trends which we are seeing in contemporary approaches to environmental management which are often piecemeal and sporadic. This approach is not consistent with the concept of sustainable development because it does not go far enough in developing strategies which will reverse the trend

41

towards environmental degradation. But the piecemeal approach is becoming the accepted ideology because it is being adopted by leading firms, espoused by academics and legitimised by standard-setters and policy makers.

## THE PERVASIVENESS OF SENIOR MANAGEMENT ETHICS

The attitudes, values and actions of senior management will tend to form the culture in any organisation. In particular, the chief executive will tend to be very important in influencing the behaviour of the next tier of executives, and down the line to the shopfloor employees. We know that senior management will tend to have a contagious influence and too often they will have a vested interest more associated with short-term performance than in acting ethically. Acting ethically and in an environmentally responsible manner therefore often requires culture change from the top down but if the chief executive is not keen to drive such change then we must ask ourselves who will?

Related to the top executive's influence over a company are the often mechanistic management systems and structures which so often exist in the most inflexible organisations. These are in place because they are easy to control, but such structures will often stifle creativity. Moreover, any discussion relating to values will be second to structure and this will too often define the firm's immediate interests in terms of short term performance. Customer and employee safety, integrity, and environmental protection will be secondary considerations.

Whilst senior management itself may not be directly involved in unethical practices, it often promotes such behaviour by strongly insisting on short-term profit maximisation and performance goals. When these goals are difficult to achieve and not achieving them can be met with severe penalties, the climate is set for undesirable conduct: deceptive advertising, overselling, adulterated products, inappropriate waste management practices, negligence towards environmental standards and other unethical behaviour. A clear alternative to the mechanistic, management dominated approach is to encourage the participation of the workforce and make them feel valued. This, in turn, encourages commitment to the organisation, better work practices and avoids problems associated with apathy and indifference (Welford, 1992).

## STRUCTURAL BARRIERS TO ETHICAL BUSINESS AND ENVIRONMENTAL MANAGEMENT

The very nature of the contemporary capitalist structure which stresses competition, the maximisation of profits and the reduction of costs acts as a fundamental barrier to the adoption of ethical practices in business. In many markets, particularly where oligopolistic structures exist, we often see strategies which are based on tacit collusion where firms will follow dominant market leaders. It is often perceived that unless such a strategy is adopted, firms will be at a competitive disadvantage and their viability may even be threatened. Therefore what becomes accepted business practice by dominant firms tends to permeate a whole industry so that the dominant ideologies associated with the most profitable companies perpetuate themselves and set the tone for business strategies. In these circumstances it is market share and financial performance which come to dominate other measures of the success of the company.

On the other hand, in times when demand falls or when any firm finds itself in a very competitive situation, financial indicators remain dominant and cost-cutting often prevails. However, we know that in two major catastrophes, Bhopal and the Alaskan oil spill, cost-cutting severely affected safety measures and contributed greatly to the gravity of the problem and the consequent handling of it (Hartley, 1993). Whatever the market structure therefore, success is measured first and foremost on principles of financial management, and wider ethical considerations are sidelined. The overemphasis on money, dictated by the economic system, therefore represents a barrier to the adoption of sustainable environmental strategies.

According to Donaldson (1989), however, the most serious barriers to improvement are not in the nature of people or business and industry, but are attitudinal. There is therefore a need to change attitudes via a change in the culture of an organisation. Central here is a commitment towards improved ethics. Many studies have demonstrated the ease with which commitment of employees can be gained through methods associated with behavioural science (Luthans, 1985). Whilst such techniques are sometimes criticised as being potentially manipulative we must recognise that they hold great potential for increasing ethical behaviour. We are, however, not seeking a bolt-on morality (so

43

often common with codes of conduct and standards) but a genuine attempt at introducing real ethical improvements.

This inevitably leads us on to considering whether current bureaucratic structures in society and in industry are conducive to the introduction of systems which promote ethical behaviour. The stunted development of any consideration of alternative forms of bureaucracy provide us with a major challenge for the future. There is a need for more innovation and imagination on the part of management. Cooperative and participative forms of industrial organisation have, for example, often been seen as appropriate only to alternative small artisan operations or have been a last resort attempt at rescuing businesses which are due to close for commercial reasons. Ethical concerns (and particularly environmental concerns) challenge us to look more closely at developments associated with industrial democracy and alternative industrial arrangements. The bureaucratic habits of hierarchy and the narrow distribution of power may not, in the end, be conducive to a sustainable future.

## OPERATIONAL BARRIERS TO ETHICAL BUSINESS AND ENVIRONMENTAL MANAGEMENT

Businesses are also prevented from acting in a more environmentally friendly way by ideologies relating to product responsibility, promotional activities and international trade which are based on custom and practice rather than any real evaluation of ethical considerations. There is an accepted code of conduct in each of these areas which, once again, stresses short term performance, perceives change as being costly and fundamentally devalues the rights of individual human beings. It is worth examining each of these issues in turn.

### Product responsibility

The traditional view of a product is that once it is sold the responsibility for its safe use and disposal passes to the consumer. That cut-off point means that firms often do not consider the environmental damage done by the use and disposal of the product which it produces. More forward-looking companies are now accepting that the product which they produce is fundamentally their responsibility from cradle to grave and the most advanced companies have introduced product stewardship procedures to ensure that a product is used correctly and disposed of in an environmentally friendly way. However, this approach is yet to be found throughout industry where the dominant ideology seems to stress the idea that property rights imply responsibility so that as soon as such rights are transferred through the sale of the product, the company no longer has a duty of care against environmental damage.

## Promotional activities

Promotional activities are designed to increase sales and are judged on the basis of so doing. The whole experience of green marketing to date has been associated with exaggeration and deception. There is often a temptation in marketing departments to exaggerate a little and to over-emphasise a product's attributes. Unfortunately, moderation is not always practised. Mild exaggerations often multiply and become outright deception. With many products, false claims can be recognised by customers, who refuse to re-buy the product. But where such claims cannot be easily substantiated false claims are harder to detect. Nevertheless pressure groups and competitors are always willing to expose unreasonable claims and that damages not only product sales but also the reputation of the firm. Advertising statements, if well presented and attractive, should induce customers to purchase the product. But, if the expectations generated by advertisements are not realised, there will be no repeat business. Repeat business is the very thing most firms seek: a continuity of business, which means loyal and satisfied customers.

## International trade

Many firms today do business worldwide and source their raw materials from a range of countries. Although this presents great opportunities, it also poses some problems, some ethical dilemmas, and many opportunities for abuse. Unethical practices have a critical effect on the image of companies at home and abroad. Union Carbide's acceptance of lower operating standards in its Third World operations led to the Bhopal accident. The lesson to be learned is that standards and controls must be even more rigidly applied in countries where workers and managers may be less competent than they are in more economically and educationally advanced countries. A major ethical question also revolves around the sourcing of raw materials from parts of the world where indigenous populations are adversely affected. The drive for low cost inputs leads to the exploitation of such people, the abuse of their land, and attacks their fundamental rights to lead their lives as they would wish.

## PROCEDURES FOR IMPROVEMENT THROUGH INDUSTRIAL DEMOCRACY

So, commonly, it is claimed that there is an inevitable trade-off between profit and ethics or morals and that the ultimate constraint to improved ethical behaviour is the need to show an acceptable rate of return on investment. The counter-claim is that behaving ethically is good business and that taking an honest and ethical approach to industrial activities will lead to satisfied customers and repeat business. The problem with both of these arguments is two-fold. Firstly, they implicitly assume that we can measure ethics and thereby characterise 'the ethical firm', or provide lists of good or bad practices. The notion of the ethical firm is not only difficult to describe but attempting so to do is also fruitless. Secondly, both arguments implicitly assume an underlying business structure where the primary outcome is profitability even though alternative models might be more applicable.

There is a need to look towards alternative ideas and alternative structures. Many of these actually require quite marginal changes but can bring about much improved outcomes. For example there are key procedures associated with reforms in the workplace which firms can adopt which will push them along the path of more ethical behaviour. This revolves around issues of industrial democracy and respecting the values of everybody associated with a firm or organisation. More open procedures and less hierarchical bureaucracy in decision making could be developed within firms. This, in turn, needs to be linked to an ethical awareness-raising campaign both within and external to the firm helping to raise the overall ethical profile.

The debate surrounding bureaucracy is too wide to go through here. But one of the most important points, and of direct relevance to the contemporary business scenario, is expounded by Argyris (1964) who argues that firms typically place individuals in positions of passivity and dependency that are at odds with the needs of mature individuals. Bennis (1972) and Burns and Stalker (1963) go further in suggesting that bureaucracies are too inflexible to be able to adapt to changes in increasingly volatile and discriminating markets. Traditional bureaucracies reserve decision making to the top of the organisation and decisions are subsequently handed down. Because of the narrow constituency involved in the decision making process, they may not only be sub-optimal decisions but may be severely at odds with the values of a workforce. Bureaucracies hold within themselves methods of controlling and channelling information. Those with power in the bureaucracy will go to great lengths to ensure conformity to internal codes and they have a great range of sanctions available to them for persuasion and enforcement. We have already argued that such codes may be at odds with more ethical behaviour. Flatter hierarchies, participative decision making and increased self determination by workers seem to be initial obvious steps to be taken to begin to resolve such problems. We will return to this assertion throughout the book.

If increased industrial democracy better enables firms to act in ethical ways and if the many advocates of participative arrangements (e.g. Welford, 1989) are right in suggesting that participation improves productivity and performance, then we need to consider why we have seen manifestation of this form of industrial organisation. Any movement towards some form of corporate democracy is taking place slowly and in a piecemeal fashion. But it might be accelerated if legislation which more freely permits different styles of participation and democratic processes was to be introduced, thus doing away with the restrictive structure of authority and responsibility required by law which often inhibits moves in this direction.

## CONCLUSIONS

Companies are faced with a challenge of integrating considerations based on the key concept of sustainable development into their production and marketing plans. There is always an incentive, however, for profit-maximising firms seeking short-term rewards, to opt out of their ethical obligations towards environmental management. What is required therefore is a thorough re-examination of business ethics within any organisation and a change in ideology towards an acceptance by industry of its ethical and social responsibilities.

Perhaps one of the most important lessons which firms are beginning to learn relates to the desirability of seeking an honest and trusting relationship with customers (as well as with their other stakeholders). Such an ethical relationship requires concern for customer satisfaction, widely defined, and fair dealings. Objectives should be written in ethical terms and stress loyalty and repeat business. Such a philosophy and attitude must permeate an organisation. It can easily be short-circuited if a general climate of opportunism and severe financial performance pressure prevail.

An honest and trusting relationship should not be sought with consumers or final users alone. It should characterise the relationship between sales representatives and their clients, which suggests no exaggeration or misrepresentation, greater efforts at understanding customers' needs, and better servicing. It may even mean forgoing a sales opportunity when a customer's best interest may be better served by another product or at another time. The trusting relationship suggests repudiating any adversarial stance with employees, with suppliers, and, beyond this, with all the communities in which a firm does business. Firms need to throw away ideologies based on financial performance alone and consider their corporate relationship with society. Such a relationship requires sound ethical conduct. It should foster a good reputation and public image.

It has been argued that the competitive nature of markets is often a barrier to corporate environmental performance, and creates isolationist strategies. Unethical and unilateral actions may result in an initial competitive advantage, but may hurt a firm's overall image and reputation in the longer term. To have a coherent environmental strategy, firms need a consistent set of business ethics and need to measure their performance using a range of longer term indicators. Placing environmental management within the framework of business ethics also reminds us that it is really not possible to separate environmental considerations from other issues such as the treatment of women and minority groups, the treatment of animals and the protection of indigenous populations. A set of ethics alone will not necessarily lead to better business practices however. What we also require is a fundamental re-examination of dominant ideologies in the business world and culture change which is capable of challenging accepted wisdoms.

The rise of organised pressure groups and interest groups makes it doubly important that managers consider the arguments of all stakeholders in a decision's outcome. Since these groups publicly promote their causes in a single-minded way and do not therefore face the competing objectives so often faced by management, they have an advantage over the traditional company in the strong message which they can convey. Decisions taken in isolation by an elite group are therefore far more likely to result in sub-optimal outcomes.

The main thrust of the argument in this chapter, however, is that the major issues and arguments surrounding business ethics, and environmental considerations in particular, are not so much substantive but more associated with procedures and received 'wisdom' associated with structures and hierarchies. It has been argued that these barriers to improved ethics can be removed through the removal of such traditional structures. There needs to be a new emphasis on stakeholder accountability and a move towards new democratic forms of organisation within the workplace. There is nothing in the nature of people or of businesses which makes adjustment towards ethical behaviour impossible. Vested interests held by those in power do have to be addressed though and this is one of the major challenges which we must overcome.

# 3

# ENVIRONMENTAL MANAGEMENT
## Systems and auditing

## INTRODUCTION

We have already indicated that there is a need for a change in the way in which the internal organisation of the firm is defined and operated. It has been suggested that new forms of ethical organisation need to be explored and that this may bring considerable benefits in moving the firm towards more sustainable patterns of business activity. However, whatever the ultimate management structure and ethos of the organisation, there will be a key role for management in binding the various parts of the organisation together and ensuring that the ultimate objectives of the organisation are realised. The next two chapters therefore outline the steps which can be taken to build a more sustainable organisation. This chapter demonstrates a need for a systemic approach to environmental management which must involve the measurement of environmental performance through auditing. It therefore outlines traditional approaches to environmental management. Chapter 4 goes beyond this to explore ecological management and strategies consistent with the achievement of sustainability at the level of the organisation.

The use of environmental management systems and of environmental auditing is now the traditional approach to corporate environmental management techniques (see, for example, Welford and Gouldson, 1993). Management systems stress the need to establish structures and norms which will ensure that environmental performance is improved over time. Few would argue that such an approach is central. However, there is more debate surrounding the methodology of the environmental audit and particularly about exactly what is measured and against which benchmark. Here the debate centres on the auditing of management systems versus more holistic approaches involving ecological auditing and auditing for sustainability (see chapter 4).

## MANAGEMENT SYSTEMS

In all parts of an organisation a systems approach to attaining the goals of the enterprise is most likely to be successful. Failure to meet such goals is often a result of an ineffective system or alternatively, that although there was a system in place, there were gaps in it which allowed mistakes and errors to occur. No matter what the structure of the firm, be it an egalitarian cooperative or a strong vertical hierarchy, it is the lack of a comprehensive and effective management system which can often lead to failure. Inadequate management systems have been the cause of environmental damage and have cost firms and organisations heavily in terms of clean-up costs and damaged reputations. At the extreme we can think of disasters such as the Exxon Valdez oil spill and the Union Carbide, Bhopal explosion, where it was the environment which became irreparably damaged due, at least in part, to inadequacies in systems which were supposed to prevent such disasters (for a review of these incidents see Welford, 1994a).

In environmental terms, at the core of the systemic approach is the role of environmental management systems where companies put into place systems and procedures which ensure that environmental performance is improved over time and that environmental damage caused by accidents does not occur. Management systems aim to pull a potentially disparate system into an integrated and organised one. To that end, the system covers not only management's responsibilities but the responsibility and tasks of every individual in an organisation.

The arguments in favour of a systems based approach are clear. A fully integrated system which covers the totality of operations helps management and workers to see their place in the organisation and recognise the interdependence of all aspects of an organisation. Through establishing clear communications, information and reporting channels it should provide a clear and understandable organisational map laying out both responsibilities and reporting arrangements. This means that functions are less likely to be overlooked and gaps in the system will not occur.

An effective management system is therefore central to the avoidance of environmental degradation, in so much as it pulls together all the other tools and strategies for the avoidance of risks and provides a framework for a clear and focused approach to environmental improvement. The management system should be developed and implemented for the purpose of accomplishing the objectives set out in a company's or organisation's policies and these must include the avoidance of environmental damage. However, it must be noted that contemporary approaches to environmental management systems depend on the central objectives and targets being set by the company itself. This has been a source of some criticism and we return to this issue again in a review of environmental management systems standards.

The management system must have three main attributes. Firstly, the system needs to be comprehensive, covering all the activities of the organisation. Gaps must not occur in the coverage of the system since this is where errors and mistakes will occur and where accidents and disasters may happen. Every part of an organisation must be involved in the implementation of the system and every person must recognise his or her responsibility for putting the system into practice.

Secondly, the system and procedures within that system need to be understandable to everybody involved. If roles and duties are not specified in an understandable way they may not be carried out. This will usually involve documenting the system, training people fully in their tasks and responsibilities and reviewing or auditing what is actually happening periodically. It requires that the system and all its elements are monitored and if the system breaks down it must be rectified quickly.

Thirdly, the system must be open to review and there must be a commitment to a continuous cycle of improvement in the operations of the firm and in the positive environmental attributes of products or services it will produce. This continuous cycle of improvement can also be applied to the environment where firms should aim for an ultimate goal of zero negative impact on the environment. Everybody has a role in the system and therefore participatory styles of management are usually superior to hierarchical ones. Management pyramids often need to be flattened to allow for a freer flow of information from both top to bottom and bottom to top.

A central aspect of any management system will revolve around decision-making. It has been argued previously that effective modern management methods will highlight the need for flexibility and worker participation and this ought to mean that decisions are taken further down any hierarchy which may exist. In arriving at decisions, the calibre and personal integrity of staff are of fundamental importance and each person in the organisation needs to understand their role in decision-making and the consequences of their actions. Decisions are often of a higher quality when they are participative and systems need to avoid giving single individuals too much power. It should also be noted that the quality of decisions will be closely linked to the availability of adequate education and training programmes for all employees and such programmes need to be built into organisation-wide systems.

The commitment of senior management to the systemic approach is crucial but real corporate change through a new environmental consensus cannot be imposed from on high. It must be developed creatively with the inner commitment of the entire workforce. There is a need to consider new styles of leadership when implementing the management system and this must be informed by systemic thinking and acting. Workers must be valued in the systemic approach and involved in decision making through participatory styles of management.

## THE TOTAL QUALITY MANAGEMENT APPROACH

The areas which are most highly developed in the context of management systems are undoubtedly in the area of quality management. It is therefore worth examining these since they do provide a powerful model for the implementation of comprehensive, understandable and open environmental management systems. For many organisations, the 1980s were a time when the benefits of quality management were recognised and where for many, new work practices, flexible arrangements and even the abandonment of production line technology were introduced. At the forefront of such innovations was the development of total quality management (TQM). TQM ultimately aims for zero-defects, that is, preventing defects occurring in the first place. For many forward-looking organisations environmental responsibility has become an aspect of the search for total quality and as such zero-defects also mean zero negative impact on the environment.

The theory behind a TQM system is that as quality improves costs actually fall through lower failure and appraisal costs and less waste. The concept that defects in the production process cost most to remedy if a product has left the factory gates seems obvious. But TQM is much more than assuring product or service quality, it is a system of dealing with quality at every stage of the production process, both internally and externally. TQM is a system requiring the commitment of senior managers, effective leadership and teamwork and this is also true of any system which aims for environmental improvements.

Traditionally, the force behind a TQM system has to come from senior management, the responsibility for quality itself belongs to everybody in the organisation and it should therefore be seen as a participatory system. The TQM system requires that every single part of the organisation is integrated and must be able to work together. This is exactly the ethos which is needed for an environmental management system to be successful; the push must come from the top but everyone has a role. For firms with a total quality management system in place or considering one the next steps towards an integrated and effective environmental management system are not hard to make.

## THE TOTAL QUALITY ENVIRONMENTAL MANAGEMENT APPROACH

Total quality environmental management (TQEM) builds on TQM and like TQM requires a systems-based approach. As a concept TQEM is more widespread in the United States but, based on the central concept of continuous improvement, it is mirrored in Europe by the eco-management and audit scheme (see below). The focus of TQEM is on shifting environmental goals from compliance to customer satisfaction. If we regard environmental damage as a quality defect then its treatment is like any other quality characteristic.

Employee involvement and participation is central to the TQEM approach. There needs to be real commitment from everybody and each employee must clearly understand their place in the organisation. Regular training to educate and train employees in improved working practices and in order to maintain the TQEM momentum is necessary. But TQEM rarely goes as far as granting employees real participatory rights, providing for industrial democracy or devolved decision making. Power structures within the organisation are usually well protected and set in stone by the documented management system.

TQEM is therefore a management-led process and requires leaders to make clear and visible the organisation's environmental values and expectations. Continuous reinforcement of such values and expectations is needed and this will require substantial personal commitment and involvement. However, we must recognise that both TQM and TQEM are long term processes. The goal is zero defects and zero pollution. That goal may never be reached and the aim is always to move ever closer to it on a continuous basis. Central to the process is customer satisfaction defined widely, and the involvement of all stakeholders. As consumers become more sophisticated in their demand for quality products which do not have a negative impact on the environment then the adoption of TQEM principles simply becomes sound business practice.

However, the focus on the consumer may also be one of the weaknesses in the TQEM approach. Customer satisfaction in the Western world is certainly not synonymous with sustainable development. Much of the problem which we see now is based on over-consumption and a wish on the part of consumers for higher and higher material standards of living. Going beyond the TQEM process and ensuring that consumers are educated and traditional attitudes are changed is fundamental to achieving sustainability. Moreover, customer satisfaction may not be consistent with the protection of ecosystems, animals and the Third World. The TQEM approach can only take us part way down the road towards sustainability, therefore, but we should see it as an initial step in the right direction.

## ENVIRONMENTAL AUDITING

Central to any management system which attempts to improve environmental performance will be the periodic environmental audit. Environmental auditing is at the centre of the systems approach to environmental management and it is worth discussing this before continuing to examine the role of management systems in general. Environmental auditing has become one of the most recent 'buzz' words to hit industry in the 1990s. It offers a methodology to evaluate the environmental performance of companies and is likely to become increasingly widespread as more and more environmental regulations and codes of practice have to be adhered to in industry.

The first environmental audits can be traced back to the United States of America, where US corporations adopted this methodology during the 1970s in response to their domestic liability laws. These were compliance audits and until the late 1980s few companies went further than this. During the 1990s some audits were extended beyond simply adhering to legislation and regulations. Proactive audits which go beyond pure compliance are slowly increasing in popularity. Such audits are more common among US industry and growing in importance in Europe. Traditionally, environmental auditing methodology has represented a series of activities initiated, by management, to evaluate environmental performance, to check compliance with environmental legislation and to assess whether the management systems in place to achieve environmental improvement are effective. This approach centres around auditing management systems. In other words, audits are done at regular intervals to assess the environmental performance of the company in relation to the company's own stated objectives, environmental policy and documented environmental management system.

Nevertheless, even this type of audit ought to be more than a simple inspection or assessment which offers an opinion based primarily on professional judgement. It has to be a methodological examination of a facility's procedures which will include analyses and testing in order to verify that legal requirements and internal policies are being met. In this context, auditors will base their judgements of compliance on evidence gathered during the audit. Neither is the audit a one-off activity. It needs to be seen as an ongoing programme where the audit is not only repeated periodically but also developed in terms of scope and sophistication over time. Seeing a single audit as a panacea would not only be wrong but is likely to lead to more problems than it solves. Central to the audit programme, therefore, is a commitment to see the process as continuous and part of a company's wide range of assessment activities.

The overall aim of environmental auditing is to gather information in order to provide an on-going status check which will enable environmental improvement within the organisation to continue and in so doing, will help to safeguard the environment and minimise the risks to life. Although auditing alone cannot achieve environmental improvement, it is a powerful managerial tool. The key objectives of the environmental audit are:

- to provide management with information in order to help them make informed decisions relating to improved environmental action;
- to determine the extent to which environmental management systems in a company are performing according to their documented procedures and aims;
- to verify compliance with local, national and European environmental and health and safety legislation, and any voluntary codes which the firm has adopted;
- to verify compliance with a company's own stated environmental policy, corporate policy and mission statement (where appropriate);
- to review the internal procedures which aim to achieve the organisation's self-determined environmental objectives and targets;
- to minimise human exposure to risks from the environment and ensure adequate health and safety provision;
- to identify and assess company risk resulting from environmental failure;
- to assess the impact on the local environment of a particular plant or process by means of air, water and soil sampling; and
- to advise a company on environmental improvements it can make and on improvements needed in the definition and/or operation of its environmental management system.

There are a number of benefits to firms in having an environmental audit undertaken. These include assurances that legislation is being adhered to and the consequent prevention of fines and litigation, an improved public image which can be built into a public relations campaign, a reduction in costs (particularly in the area of energy usage and waste minimisation), an improvement in environmental awareness at all levels of the firm and an improvement in overall quality. But many environmental audit programmes are still established on the direct orders of top management for the purpose of identifying the compliance status of individual facilities and thereby providing management with a sense of security that environmental requirements are being met. Whilst this is good practice, it leaves open to question the issue as to whether the traditional auditing process is really identifying the key elements and measures required to move an organisation towards sustainability.

The primary benefits of environmental auditing are to indicate in good time whether environmental measures are satisfactory and to assist with the subsequent compliance with legislation, company policy and the public's demands. Experience of auditing has highlighted additional benefits. For example, we have already stressed the need for increased worker participation a number of times before. Because it is an information gathering exercise at all levels of the organisation, the process of auditing increases awareness of environmental policies and responsibilities amongst the whole workforce and provides management with an opportunity to give credit for good environmental performance.

An increasing number of consultancies have been established during the late 1980s and 1990s which aim to undertake environmental audits. Some of these have grown out of quality assurance operations and others out of the expertise developed through environmental impact assessment. However, environmental auditing requires skills and attributes which go beyond both of these frameworks and entails a much more interdisciplinary approach.

Increasingly some degree of external help and consultancy will be needed by business for a number of reasons. Firstly, all but the largest of firms are unlikely to have the necessary expertise to cover the legal, scientific and technical and management related requirements of the audit process. Secondly, companies are increasingly looking for third party verification of their audit results. External consultants can bring a degree of objectivity to the process and introduce fresh ideas. Thirdly, many audits have traditionally been site specific and have not sought to assess external environmental effects of operations. There is, however, a clear trend towards an assessment of external environmental effects such as pollution and disamenities where expertise and measurement beyond a single plant or operation are required. Finally, the findings of audits were traditionally for internal company consumption but there is now a move by some companies, reacting to demands from pressure groups and encouragement from industry itself, government and the EU, to publish the results more widely and to consider the provision of public information. Thus the information resulting from the audit needs to be comprehensible to the public and believed by them. This can be achieved with external impartial advice and third party verification.

Over the last decade, as public attitudes towards environmental degradation have changed, as insurance markets have become more aware of the potential risks associated with pollution and as more national and transnational legislation has come on to the statute book the incentives to undertake an environmental audit have increased. The reasons for undertaking the environmental audit are therefore likely to include the following considerations.

Costs of remediation following pollution incidents have been increasing dramatically and consequently premiums have increased and the number of exclusions from policies has extended. Whilst it is still possible to find insurance cover for pollution which is sudden, accidental and unforeseen, there are very few insurance companies which will cover general pollution risks unless an environmental audit has been carried out.

One of the consequences of public interest is that consumers are increasingly willing to switch to products which are in some way more environmentally friendly than their normal purchase. Companies need therefore to demonstrate that their product and their processes cause minimum harm to the environment. In the past the marketing of 'green' products has often been misleading and sometimes dishonest and many firms have had their 'green' products exposed as not being environmentally friendly at all. With the growing strength of pressure groups, dishonesty will be exposed and it is therefore necessary for firms who wish to tell their consumers about their environmental improvements to undertake independent environmental audits of their processes. With the introduction of an eco-label for some products across Europe which will assess not only the product but the production process before an award is made, the role of the audit becomes crucial.

Major organisations are becoming increasingly aware of the massive potential risks involved in acquiring land which has already been contaminated or acquiring a business which has poor environmental performance. Costs associated with ground remediation, the capital cost associated with introducing or upgrading pollution control plant and the cost of potential compensation claims for past mistakes can easily outweigh any financial advantage of an acquisition. It is increasingly standard practice, therefore, to commission a pre-acquisition environmental assessment.

Environmental legislation in Europe and America increasingly requires organisations to reduce emissions to the atmosphere and discharges to rivers and sewers using methods which present the best environmental option (BEO) and the best available technology or techniques. In many countries specific industries involved in the processing of toxic materials have, in addition, to apply to a government agency for an authorisation to operate. Applications for such authorisation, which are likely to be expanded in the future, often require the completion of a complex questionnaire and this is sometimes not possible without the information which results from an environmental audit.

## THE TRADITIONAL METHODOLOGY OF ENVIRONMENTAL AUDITING

All environmental audits involve gathering information, analysing that information, making objective judgements based on evidence and a knowledge of the industry and of environmental legislation and standards, and reporting the results to senior management with recommendations and possible strategies for the implementation of the findings. The traditional approach places an emphasis on the auditing of the environmental management system and an assessment that the organisation is meeting its self-defined policy objectives and targets. There are three stages to an audit.

The first stage, the pre-audit stage, will aim to minimise the time spent at the site and to maximise the audit team's productivity and will involve:

1 Planning the nature and scope of the audit and providing a framework for setting goals and objectives, developing strategies for their achievement and specifying accountability for accomplishing the work and scheduling the audit process.
2 Selecting members of the audit team and allocating resources to the strategies and policies determined in 1. The audit team will consist of people chosen for their expertise not only in environmental matters but also having knowledge of the industry in which a company operates. An assignment of audit responsibilities should be made according to the competencies and experience of the team.
3 Getting to know the industry and company to be audited. A useful strategy here is to use pre-survey questionnaires submitted to management in order for the audit team to familiarise

themselves with the type of instalment, the site and the location. It will also focus the minds of management on what will be required of them during the audit.

4 Questionnaires may also be sent to a representative sample of the workforce (to be filled out in confidence) asking about key issues such as communications, planning, health and safety and working conditions.

The second stage is the on-site audit itself. This will include:

5 An inspection of records kept by the company, certificates of compliance, discharge consents, waste licences, etc.

6 The examination of inspection and maintenance programmes and the company's own policy on what to do in the event of spills and other accidents. Auditors will have to assess the soundness of the facility's internal controls and assess the risks associated with the failure of those controls. Such controls will include management procedures and the equipment and engineering controls that affect environmental performance.

7 Examining lines of management and responsibility, competence of personnel and systems of authorisation. There needs to be a working understanding of the facility's internal management system and of its effectiveness.

8 A confidential interview of selected staff at all levels of operation with a view to collecting information, particularly in the area of the effectiveness of systems and waste management.

9 A physical inspection of the plant, working practices, office management systems and surrounding areas including a check on safety equipment, verifying the company's own sampling and monitoring procedures, investigating energy management systems and where necessary taking samples of waste, liquids, soil, air and noise.

The final stage of the audit will involve:

10 Confirming that there is sufficient evidence on which to base and justify a set of findings and evaluating the audit information and observations. Such evaluation will involve the audit team meeting to discuss all facets of the environmental audit.

11 Reporting the audit findings in written form and in discussion with the management of the audited company. This entails a formal review of the audit findings to avoid misinterpretation and discussion about how to improve the environmental per-

formance of the firm based on the audit report. Management is thus provided with information about compliance status and recommendations regarding action which should be taken.

12 This will often result in the development of an action plan to address deficiencies. This will include assigning responsibilities for corrective action, determining potential solutions and establishing timetables. Recommendations for the next audit may also be made.

Whilst we have outlined a generic model of an environmental audit, we have not discussed in any detail exactly what would be measured and what information would be gathered. Much debate centres around the extent to which auditing must go beyond the assessment of the effectiveness of the system alone. The most common approach to this is typified by the increasingly popular environmental management systems standards where systems and environmental impacts are assessed. It is to the systems standards we now turn, but we will return to the debate surrounding exactly what to audit in the next chapter.

## ENVIRONMENTAL MANAGEMENT SYSTEMS AND STANDARDS

Once they are in place, management systems should satisfy the objectives for which they were introduced. Increasingly, firms will wish to tell their customers and suppliers about their management system and achieve recognised levels of management practice. For this reason and others, as outlined below, firms are often building their own management system to conform with some pre-determined standards laid down by outside agencies. Responsible Care (discussed in chapter 2), BS5750 (ISO9000), BS7750 and the European eco-management and audit scheme are examples of such standards.

Like the measurement and specification of materials and products, the standardisation of quality systems has become increasingly important. In the last decade, one British Standard has attracted overwhelming attention. BS5750 was the world's first published national standard dealing with a complete approach to quality management. Internationally, BS5750 is the basis of the European Quality Standard EN29000 and of the ISO9000 series. Following the philosophy of BS5750 environmental management systems will also become standardised, measured and accredited via BS7750. Such standards set down technical and sometimes organisational criteria which help to:

- ensure that goods and services are fit for the purpose and meet a customer's needs;
- rationalise, simplify and harmonise manufacturing techniques thus reducing needless variety and duplication or misuse of resources;
- provide a means of communication and measurement which can be used in the specification of contracts;
- provide a means of communication and identification to customers and suppliers;
- ensure safety and good health.

## BS7750

BS7750, the British Standards Institution's (BSI) standard on environmental management systems was launched in 1992 after over a year's discussion with industry and practitioners. Subsequent to a pilot programme its final version was published in 1994. The standard provides a management tool increasingly demanded by a range of stakeholders from consumers to shareholders. It is the first of a new generation of standards covering every aspect of environmental management. Similar systems standards have been published in Ireland, Spain and Canada and these will form the basis of an international standard on environmental management systems.

Introducing a standard for environmental management was a significant milestone in industry's acceptance of its need to internalise its environmental effects. As the standard is increasingly adopted it will cease to be part of a company's strategy for creating a 'competitive edge' and will become a minimum standard for good practice. The standard is designed to aid industry by providing a generic model that will help organisations to establish, develop and maintain their own purpose-built environmental management system.

The standard does not attempt to outline expected levels of environmental performance or minimum expected levels of pollution control. This has resulted in some criticism of the standard. Many argue that some minimum performance measure should have been introduced. Quite what that measure would be is less clear. Indeed, the whole issue of the measurement of environmental performance is an area where considerable research is required. Since performance criteria are not specified, compliance with the standard is centred on the ability of the organisation to meet its own stated objectives. Those objectives will change and be modified over time providing for constant improvement of environmental impacts. Central to the system is the recognition of the need for regular auditing and a continuous cycle of improvement.

Central to the organisation adopting the standard is a commitment to control its environmental performance and the first step is therefore to undertake an environmental review (sometimes referred to as a baseline environmental audit) and formulate a coherent policy statement. All activities have to be recorded, assessed and audited and product development has to be examined in terms of a rather loose life cycle analysis.

The system adopted by the organisation has to be documented and subsequent activities have to adhere to that system and performance has to be measured. In the light of experience the stated policy has to be reconsidered and the whole process repeats itself. Therefore adherence to the standard should bring about improvement over time. However, the extent of that improvement will be determined by the objectives and targets set by the organisation itself. Where these are ambitious and challenging, considerable improvement can occur. Where they are not, however, any change will be marginal and inherently piecemeal. Such an approach would seem to be hardly ethical and inconsistent with sustainability.

Companies which have been through a BS5750 (ISO9000) development process will find BS7750 relatively easy to implement to the extent that much of the system documentation required is parallel to that required under BS5750. Nevertheless like BS5750, the documentation requirements for BS7750 can be formidable. That documentation is central to certification, however, since the standard puts most stress on the system being in place and the adherence to self-imposed objectives. The documentation therefore provides the evidence to the certifier.

The standard is designed to be applicable to a wide range of industries from manufacturing to service organisations. Central to its requirement is the need to consider the total organisation and the total process which means that the environmental management system can be based on many of the techniques and principles of total quality management. In addition, organisations should also be seen as being involved in a wider process flow where they will have impacts beyond the boundaries of their own production process. For example the use of raw materials and the disposal of products after use are, to some extent, influenced by the organisation, and life cycle assessment represents an appropriate tool for the analysis of wider product impacts. )

The standard is fully compatible with European Union initiatives on environmental management and eco-labelling and has its own system of certification for compliance. The key requirements of BS7750, summarised by Welford and Gouldson (1993) are as follows:

1 Environmental policy. BS7750 requires that the environmental management system (EMS) should aim to ensure compliance with the environmental policy and objectives of the firm. At an early stage therefore there is a need for a clear and detailed consideration of what that policy should be. It must be seen as an integral part of the EMS and stress the need for a continuous cycle of environmental improvement. The policy must nevertheless be understandable and communicated widely to ensure implementation at every level of the organisation.

2 Commitment. The standard requires commitment at the highest level in the company. By adopting the standard an organisation will have to accept the changes which this implies and support for change is therefore required at Board level. Management needs to publicly declare its wholehearted support for the adoption of the standard.

3 Environmental review. There is a need for organisations to carry out an initial environmental review which will provide the information required to design the organisation's environmental management system. The Standard document lays out a whole range of suggested areas for investigation.

4 Organisation. Personnel are central to the success of any management system and jobs and roles within the organisation must be clearly defined and their links with each other made apparent. People must be clear about their own role, the authority with which to act and their lines of demarcation, responsibility and reporting. The organisation must therefore be tight. Gaps in an organisational structure are often the source of mistakes and problems.

5 Registers of environmental effects. Organisations are required to keep registers of environmental legislation, regulations, planning requirements and discharge consents relevant to their operations. They must also develop an effects register which evaluates the environmental impacts of their operations based on a life cycle approach from procurement to disposal of products after use.

6 Objectives and targets. Organisations should specify attainable and achievable targets which nevertheless go beyond minimum legislatory requirements. The targets can be staged over predefined timescales to achieve a continuous cycle of improvement.

7 Environmental management programme, records and documentation. Plans and strategies to achieve environmental improvement must be clearly defined and documented. Procedures and responsibilities must be defined in detail and there must be procedures for adapting and changing the plan in the light of changing requirements, results of the environmental audit and experience. There must be systems in place for maintaining records relevant to the environmental strategy. These must include records of any failure of compliance and information concerning suppliers and contractors. More detailed consideration of documentation is provided below.

8 Operational controls and records. There must be measurement and verification of the organisation's activities and the effectiveness of its strategies for environmental improvement. If measurement discovers the failure to meet specific targets then procedures for corrective action must be defined.

9 Environmental audits. Organisations must carry out periodic audits of the operations and systems based on a detailed and documented plan setting out the auditing methodology and the procedures for reporting and publishing findings.

10 System reviews. Management systems should be open to adaptation and refinement based on the results of the auditing exercise and experience and there must be a commitment to periodic reviews of the environmental management system and its operation.

The environmental management system must be designed by the company around these general requirements. In effect, this means that the organisation must design, implement and continuously improve processes aimed at achieving the objectives and targets laid out in the environmental policy. BS7750 does provide a generic model on which to build the specific design which requires processes to be put in place to ensure that:

- a policy exists and is properly communicated;
- management responsibilities are clearly defined, properly organised and have appropriate resources allocated to them;
- education and training programmes exist;
- inventories exist of the environmental effects of the organisation;
- inventories exist of the legal requirements;
- the objectives and specific targets to be attained are clearly stated and that these are drawn from the results of the environmental review and the organisation's stated policy;
- a plan of how the targets are to be met is established;
- appropriate quality control systems are in place to ensure compliance with the plans;
- appropriate records are kept;
- regular audits are carried out to ensure that the system works and continuous improvement can be achieved.

The actual design of the system will have to be periodically reviewed by management based on the information supplied by the audit and changing legislative requirements and stakeholder pressure. The approach must at all times be systematic and documented.

There are four central elements of the environmental management system. These are the environmental review, the environmental policy, the system itself in terms of its design and implementation, and the environmental audit. Let us deal with each element in turn:

### a. The environmental review

BS7750 requires that environmental effects inventories are kept. One of these should record the actual impact of an organisation's activities on the environment and the initial environmental review is therefore the baseline for establishing this and will be the level against which improvements are measured. It is therefore critical that the results of the review are documented. Much of the documentation at this early stage will simply represent an inventory of the organisation's activities.

67

If we build on this idea of inventory analysis the documentation might include:

1 Consumption inventory. This would record all materials consumed by the organisation over a particular time period often broken down into generalised categories with particular attention paid to natural resources and hazardous substances.

2 Product inventory. A listing of all products produced by the company over the same time period which might include some analysis of the life cycle impact of the products.

3 Releases inventory. A listing of all releases to the air and water including particulate releases and an assessment of the impact of these activities.

4 Disposal inventory. All materials which are disposed of should be recorded along with details of how they are disposed of with particular attention being paid to the ratio between on-site disposal and off-site disposal.

5 Stocks inventory. A listing of stocks kept over the period paying particular attention to hazardous substances and the potential risks of the stockholding and any warehousing entailed.

6 Reconciliation. The first five inventories should be capable of reconciliation in terms of mass balance. This exercise helps to discover undetected waste and emissions.

7 Impacts inventory. An assessment of the overall impact on the environment should be made. This should cover site-specific, local, regional and global impacts and pay particular attention to impacts on local communities.

8 Impact mechanisms. The routes by which impacts occur are important and should be identified and recorded. The analysis should cover procurement, life cycle impact of products, processes, storage, transport, waste disposal and emissions and accidents. A clear understanding of impact mechanisms is required in order to attempt to reduce the level of such impacts.

9 Regulatory and legislative requirements register. A record of all regulations, legislation, planning requirements, etc. pertinent to the operation of the organisation should be kept. These will be treated as a minimum level of compliance and suggestions may be made for going beyond these minimum requirements.

10 The existing management system. The review needs to identify the extent to which a systematic management system already

exists within the organisation and the good and bad practices which arise from this. Where a recognised standard such as BS5750 has been implemented some consideration of how BS7750 might be implemented in parallel needs to be undertaken.

## b. The environmental policy

The organisation must have a clear and detailed policy with respect to environmental improvement. This should be widely available and at least a summary of it should be available to the public. The method by which the policy is to be made available to the whole organisation, along with measures taken to ensure that the policy has been understood and is being acted upon must be documented. Where a policy sets specific objectives for each of its general impacts then these should be explained and justified and shown to be realistic, yet ambitious and attainable.

## c. System design and implementation

The plan of the environmental system needs to be set out in considerable detail and both its design (in terms of structure) and its implementation strategy need to be considered. It must be made clear how the environmental management system sets out to achieve the objectives set out in the policy statement.

The documentation for the EMS needs to lay out how it proposes to achieve its objectives and would typically cover:

- staff responsibilities, standard lines of reporting and procedures for unforeseen circumstances such as accidents;
- the resources to be devoted to the EMS, a justification of these and a demonstration of how these resources will bring about environmental improvement;
- specific actions to be undertaken by the organisation to meet specific environmental objectives along with a timescale for implementation;
- a timetable of anticipated environmental achievements and details of how these are to be measured and assessed, and procedures for action should the targets not be met;
- the way in which staff are to be informed of their specific tasks in the organisation which may include the production and

distribution of manuals and other documentation setting out roles and responsibilities;

- the way in which staff are to be trained in new working practices, new procedures or general environmental awareness, the content of the training programmes and what they seek to achieve;
- the coordination and management of all the organisation's activities related to its environmental performance;
- a clear mechanism by which environmental performance will be monitored and a justification of that system;
- a schedule, protocol and methodology for regularly auditing the performance of the environmental management system and the environmental performance of the organisation;
- the mechanism by which all results and assessments will be verified;
- a schedule for regular strategic reviews of the organisation's policy and environmental management system;
- the way in which the organisation will communicate its environmental performance to its stakeholders.


### d. The environmental audit

The environmental audit should compare the organisation's actual environmental performance against basic standards set by legislation and regulations, the organisation's own stated objectives and by best practice elsewhere (for example by a company's competitors). The documentation for the EMS needs to establish a clear auditing methodology including the timing of the auditing procedure.

The standard specifies that the organisation shall establish and maintain procedures for audits to be carried out, in order to determine:

- whether or not environmental management activities conform to the environmental management programme, and are implemented effectively;
- the effectiveness of the environmental management system in fulfilling the organisation's environmental policy.

For this purpose, the organisation must establish and maintain an audit plan which will deal with the following points.

1 The specific activities and areas to be audited, which include:

> organisational structures;
> administrative and operational procedures;
> work areas, operations and processes;
> documentation, reports and records;
> environmental performance.

2 The frequency of auditing of each activity/area, audits being scheduled on the basis of the nature and environmental importance of the activity concerned, and the results of previous audits.
3 The responsibility for auditing each activity/area.
4 The personnel requirements, and specifically that those carrying out the audits:

> are independent, so far as it is possible, of the specific activities or areas being audited;
> have experience in relevant disciplines;
> have support, where necessary, from a wider range of specialists, who may be internal or external to the organisation.

5 The protocol for conducting the audits, which may involve the use of questionnaires, checklists, interviews, measurements and direct observations, depending on the nature of the function being audited.
6 The procedures for reporting audit findings to those responsible for the activity/area audited, who shall take timely action on reported deficiencies. Reporting shall address:

> conformity or nonconformity of the environmental management system elements with specified requirements;
> the effectiveness of the implemented environmental management system in meeting objectives and targets;
> implementation and effectiveness of any corrective actions recommended in previous audits;
> conclusions and recommendations.

7 The procedures for publishing audit findings, if the organisation has such a commitment.

It is important to note therefore that the primary function of the audit will be to assess compliance or non-compliance with legislation and the company's own stated objectives and targets and to check that the environmental management system is working.

Therefore what is measured, how it is measured and over what timescale, will all be determined by the need to gather the relevant information to meet this limited and somewhat narrow function. Implicitly wide-ranging environmental audits which go beyond the self-imposed objectives and targets are not required. The bulk of auditing within this standard is therefore systems auditing and detailed ecological impacts of a company's operations do not have to be part of the audit. This has to be seen as a major weakness.

## THE EUROPEAN ECO-MANAGEMENT AND AUDIT SCHEME

Back in 1990 the Environment Directorate of the (then) European Community began discussions about an eco-auditing scheme. Initial proposals were that over fifty industrial sectors would be covered by a mandatory scheme whereby companies within those sectors would be required to undertake annual environmental audits and publish a detailed environmental statement. After considerable pressure from industry and debate surrounding the costs of imposing such a scheme the requirements were relaxed and the mandatory nature of the scheme was abandoned.

At the end of 1991 the European Commission approved a proposal for a Council Regulation to establish a European Community audit scheme which would be open for voluntary participation by industrial companies. The final Regulation establishing the eco-management and audit scheme was published in 1993. The scheme provides a framework for companies to think ahead, assess their own environmental impacts and commit themselves to a policy of reducing them. It also encourages firms to keep the public informed by regularly making statements and reporting progress. The eco-management and audit scheme is voluntary and administered by individual Member States but many argue that the scheme should become compulsory for larger firms and the Council has retained the right to introduce compulsory registration in chosen industries. Member States themselves also have the right to adopt a compulsory registration system for certain industrial categories if they feel this is beneficial. The scheme applies to industrial sites but provision is made within the scheme to experiment with its application in non-industrial organisations.

The objective of the eco-management and audit scheme is to

promote improvements in the environmental performance of industry by requiring companies to:

- establish and implement environmental policies, programmes and management systems on a site-specific basis;
- carry out periodic, systematic and objective evaluations of activities through an environmental audit; and to
- provide information about environmental performance to the public.

The purpose of the scheme is not to confirm compliance with legislative requirements (although this must be achieved), nor is it aimed at awarding best practice or performance. Like BS7750, the scheme aims to recognise efforts to improve environmental performance over time, given a baseline established by an environmental review of the firm. Thus the scheme highlights the need for a continuous cycle of improvement.

Essentially there are seven stages to be undertaken by those sites wishing to register with the scheme. The firm must:

1 adopt an environmental policy;
2 undertake an environmental review;
3 establish environmental programmes;
4 install an environmental management system;
5 undertake an environmental audit;
6 prepare an environmental statement; and
7 seek verification.

Central to the scheme is the need to conduct regular environmental audits therefore. Like BS7750, the audit assesses this system and evaluates performance in relation to the environmental review and the operation of the system as defined and documented. The results of the audit have to be considered by senior management and any necessary revisions to the company policy, objectives, targets, action plans and systems made.

All of these steps can be internal to the company if there is sufficient expertise available to perform the various tasks adequately. Indeed the intention of the eco-management and audit scheme is that the discipline of having to follow these steps should help the company better manage its own environmental performance.

The eco-management and audit scheme requires that an external environmental statement is prepared based on the findings of the audit or initial review. Validation of this statement must be made by external accredited environmental verifiers. The validation will confirm that the statement has covered all of the environmental issues relevant to the site in enough detail and that the information presented is reliable. The validation process involved the examination of relevant documentation, including information about the site, its activities, a description of the environmental management system and details and findings of the environmental review or audit. This would normally be followed by an inspection visit to the site and preparation of a verifier's report.

In order to register under the eco-management and audit scheme a company has to be able to demonstrate that this sequence of events has taken place, and that sensible targets have been set towards which the firm should make progress. The approved independent and accredited environmental verifier (AEV) will have checked that the audit process was carried out properly and that the environmental report is a true and fair view of the company's environmental performance.

## LINKAGES BETWEEN BS7750 AND THE ECO-MANAGEMENT AND AUDIT SCHEME

The development of BS7750 began when the EU scheme was a proposed eco-audit scheme, focusing on auditing environmental performance against undefined criteria. Within the UK it was felt essential that any audit programme should have an object against which to carry out an audit, a statement or standard of some kind. The object chosen was the environmental management system as defined by BS7750.

Gilbert (1994) suggests that as a familiar approach used by many in UK industry, BS7750 provides a key stepping stone towards full participation in the eco-management and audit scheme. There is one significant difference; there is no requirement to publish audit results of environmental performance to meet the requirements of BS7750. This allows organisations to establish an EMS, assess progress and results before taking the key step to publication of performance. Not surprisingly many firms feel safer in keeping the results of their investigations into environmental performance a secret.

## PROBLEMS WITH THE BS7750 AND ECO-MANAGEMENT AND AUDITING APPROACHES

The most cited criticism of the BS7750 approach and implicit within the eco-management and audit scheme is that basic environmental performance requirements are not specified. Instead, compliance with the standard is centred on each firm specifying and reaching its own performance objectives and hence even the most environmentally damaging firms will be able to achieve BS7750 and the prestige that may come with it, so long as they can demonstrate the existence of a management system which can deliver incremental environmental improvement. In other words the only requirement seems to be to demonstrate a capability for marginal environmental improvements within a self-determined framework of policies, targets, systems and assessment methodologies.

The ability of firms to set themselves targets that are honest and realistic yet challenging and attainable, and result in significant (as opposed to incremental) improvements in environmental performance will ultimately be the benchmark against which the efficacy of the voluntary approach is measured. The standards are backed by industry possibly because voluntary action is perceived to be less costly than compliance with regulations, and they are considered to be easily achievable. Moreover, when other corporate objectives (e.g. profitability) are under pressure, the voluntary approach allows for a loosening up of other (perhaps secondary) objectives (Shayler et al., 1994).

Effectively, the standards are designed to certify appropriate environmental management systems rather than efficient environmental management. The never-ending cycle of assessment should mean that the firm is continually learning from its mistakes and successes. But the speed of environmental improvement is dependent upon the targets that the organisation sets itself and these might represent environmental tokenism rather than a solid commitment to decreasing environmental impact in some cases.

However, the introduction of any integrated environmental management system should be welcomed. It acknowledges that an environmental strategy is more than an add-on to other corporate policies and is actually central to good business management. Together with the EU eco-management and audit scheme, BS7750 represents a major step forward in harmonising and formalising environmental management practices. However, neither BS7750 nor the EU scheme really acknowledge the importance to companies of recognising and comprehending the rapid evolution of environmental issues within the broader concept of sustainable development.

The preliminary findings of the BS7750 pilot programme indicated a number of difficulties with the standard. One common problem reported was that companies were generally strong on drawing up environmental policies and carrying out preliminary reviews, but weak on providing training and resources and setting environmental targets (ENDS, 1993a). This is potentially serious as these areas are the most important in establishing an improvement in environmental performance rather than simply taking note of the company's present position. A further problem that may have implications for the integration of environmental strategy within overall business strategy was that environmental managers have had difficulty in persuading board members to consider environmental issues (ENDS, 1993a). However, a number of firms (including Texaco, Rolls Royce and United Engineering Steels) have found that BS7750 has helped them to build more strategic environmental policies. The preliminary environmental review in particular was described as an 'eye opener' (ENDS, 1993b).

## CONCLUSIONS

Environmental management means many things to many people, but it is best categorised according to what it represents in current practice in industry. In other words we must see environmental management in the context of an approach which parallels total quality management, adopting a management systems approach with a central role for auditing methodologies. Environmental management systems standards are a natural extension of this type of approach and potentially have a central role to play in establishing environmental management systems within general business strategy. But self-imposed environmental objectives and targets devalue the standards and do little to guarantee a sustainable future. Goals need to be set by an independent regulatory body and independent accreditation is essential. It must always be remembered that the standards address environmental management systems and not environmental management more widely defined.

However, there are wider issues to be addressed as well. These revolve around the need to move swiftly towards a sustainable future. Neither BS7750 nor the EU eco-management and audit scheme provide a real consideration of the principles of sustainable development. That is not to suggest that current environmental management practice is necessarily bad. They provide principles which all firms should work towards. The issue is whether they go far enough. The EU scheme is clearly superior to BS7750 because of its requirement for third party verification and reporting via the environmental statement but it is still overtly management-system driven.

We return to a common theme therefore. That is that the key concept of sustainable development requires a new approach to business. We have seen little evidence of a radical paradigm shift either in the eco-management and auditing or the BS7750 standards. A responsible and proactive approach to the environment requires new and radical approaches to doing business. In its present form a standard like BS7750 could be viewed as a new pawn in a non-price competition strategy and hence give a perceived advantage to those who can afford its implementation. Therefore the release of the standard in a period of widespread recession could be seen as something worse than just bad timing. As other pressures on firms increase, environmental issues are likely to become less important due to the legislation aimed at enforcing environmental consideration.

Rethinking business strategy along the lines of sustainable development does require a change in the culture of an organisation and it therefore opens up new opportunities to reassess other aspects of business. Traditional approaches to environmental auditing are now being superseded by new approaches more firmly based around the ideas of deep ecology and sustainable development and these are the types of strategy to which we now turn.

# 4

# BEYOND ENVIRONMENTAL MANAGEMENT
## Deep ecology and sustainability

### INTRODUCTION

We found in chapter 3 that traditional approaches to environmental management were bounded by traditional approaches to business and were therefore somewhat restricted. In particular, it was suggested that environmental management practices tended to parallel quality management, that systems management was stressed, meaning that ecological concerns are not fully internalised, and that environmental management systems standards left it to industry to set their own environmental performance targets.

In this chapter, whilst we accept the need for a systemic approach to management we go beyond the traditional paradigm, breaking down the traditional links between quality and the environment, and examine the contribution which the concepts of deep ecology and sustainable development can make. To that end we move beyond environmental management towards ecological management and sustainability management. This takes the firm down the road of a more holistic approach to doing business. It argues that the firm cannot exist in isolation but is an important social and economic agent which has an important role to play in shaping future society.

### BREAKING THE LINK BETWEEN QUALITY AND THE ENVIRONMENT

Many commentators, including earlier work of this author, have stressed what they see as natural linkages between quality management and the improvement of environmental performance (see for example, Welford, 1992, or Welford and Gouldson, 1993). It has been argued that this link exists through the need for environmental management systems and their associated auditing procedures, and that the general approach taken in philosophies such as total quality management mirror the desired approach for environmental improvement. The aim of both approaches is to achieve a continuous cycle of improvement through the commitment of everybody involved in an organisation.

This same link has led to the development of BS7750 and the eco-management and audit scheme. Such standards have been heralded as the major step forward which will provide incentives for businesses to improve their environmental performance. Fundamental to both schemes is a need to develop an environmental management system (EMS) and to undertake periodic audits of undefined measures of environmental performance and the management system itself. Both standards specify incremental environmental improvement as their aim rather than the achievement of a clearly defined threshold below which firms may not fall. In parallel with this, whilst the environmental auditing methodology which has been based on the management system approach does provide for continuous improvement, it also means that major polluters who are producing extremely unsustainable products are able to gain the award and the prestige which such a badge brings them. Moreover, we know from the experience of ISO9000 (BS5750), that certificates of compliance are often pinned to the wall and subsequently forgotten about until the auditors are due again. There is no reason to suppose that the same will not happen with BS7750 and the eco-management and audit scheme, and rather than provide for environmental improvement, that may lead to environmental negligence by the very firms which have been accredited by the 'highest' standards.

If we go back to some of the most important writings on corporate environmental strategy, we find that quality management approaches were never given the same emphasis which they have developed more recently. Environmental management systems were originally conceptualised as comprehensive systems in their own right and did not parallel quality management paradigms. The most cited of these comprehensive systems has been the 'integrated system of ecologically conscious management' developed by Georg Winter, known simply today as the Winter model.

Winter (1987) lists six reasons why any responsible manager should implement the principles of ecologically conscious management. In a translation by Callenbach *et al.* (1993) these are:

1 Human survival: without ecologically conscious companies, we cannot achieve an ecologically conscious economy; without an ecologically conscious economy, human survival will be endangered.

2 Public consensus: without ecologically conscious companies, there will be no public consensus with the business community; without such consensus, the market economy would be in political jeopardy.

3 Market opportunities: without ecologically conscious management, there will be a loss of fast-growing market opportunities.

4 Reduction of risks: without ecologically conscious management, companies face risks of liability for environmental damages, potentially involving enormous sums of money and personal liabilities of directors, executives and other staff members.

5 Reduction of costs: without ecologically conscious management, there will be a loss of numerous opportunities for cost reductions.

6 Personal integrity: without ecologically conscious management, both managers and employees will sense a lack of personal integrity and thus be unable to fully identify with their jobs.

Winter goes on to lay out six principles that are considered essential for the long term success of a responsibly managed company:

1 Quality: a product is of high quality only if it is manufactured in an environmentally benign way and if it can be used and disposed of without causing environmental damage.

2 Creativity: the creativity of the company's workforce is enhanced by working conditions that respect human biological needs.

3 Humaneness: the general working atmosphere will be more humane if the corporate goals and strategies are geared not only towards economic success but also towards a sense of responsibility with regard to all forms of life.

4 Profitability: the company's profitability can be increased by adopting cost-reducing ecological innovations and by exploiting market opportunities for ecologically appealing products.

5 Continuity: in the interest of the company's continuity, it is

becoming more and more important to avoid liability risks under increasingly stringent environmental regulation and market risks resulting from the decreasing demand for environmentally damaging products.

6 Loyalty: ultimately, the staff of a company will be loyal to their country and fellow citizens only if they are emotionally attached to it, which will only happen so long as the country has not lost its character through environmental destruction.

Thus the Winter model stresses the strategic use of traditional management tools for ecological purposes. Issues of quality are part of the model rather than running parallel to it and dictating its method and focus. Winter puts much more emphasis on issues such as job satisfaction, valuing the employee and a sense of responsibility to all forms of life. Moreover, the Winter model is not a model founded on the concept of 'business as usual'. It stresses creativity amongst management and employees. According to Dyllik (1989) the vehicles of such creativity are innovation, cooperation and communication as defined below:

- Innovation: in contrast to traditional capital and labour saving innovations, ecologically conscious strategies require resource-conserving innovations which may be of two kinds: those reducing the environmental impact of the company's operation and those providing the consumer with ecological advantages.
- Cooperation: the importance of cooperation amongst all stakeholders throughout the life cycle of a product derives from the fact that economic and ecological effects obey different laws. Whereas competition is the guiding principle of the former, cooperation is central to the latter.
- Communication: in traditional management strategies, communication and public relations are understood as components of marketing and restricted to product or image publicity. In ecologically conscious management strategies, by contrast, the task of communication acquires overall strategic importance, due to the crisis of confidence affecting individual companies and entire industries.

Such an approach which emphasises creativity goes beyond the traditional paradigm of environmental management. It extends the quality management approach into new areas for consideration and puts much more emphasis on ecology rather than economy.

We have argued therefore that an approach which puts stress on the quality approach which, in turn, is based on management systems aimed at continuous improvement, is a reasonable starting point. But there is a need to go beyond this approach (or indeed go back to some of the original writings on ecological management). Linking quality and the environment is an approach which is fundamentally enshrined in the marginalist reform approaches identified as inadequate in chapter 1.

## ENVIRONMENTAL MANAGEMENT AND ECOLOGICAL MANAGEMENT

We saw in chapter 3 that, because of the way environmental management has been interpreted by industry, it has increasingly become a defensive and piecemeal approach which does not break away from any of the dominant paradigms of traditional profit-centred business. Ecological management on the other hand is more proactive, more creative and demands that we reassess some of the 'sacred tenets' of the capitalist system. Ecological management is founded in the work of Winter (1987) but extended to include aspects of deep ecology.

Lutz (1990) argues that we must recognise that the world's ecological problems cannot be understood in isolation. They are systemic problems which are interdependent and interconnected and need a new kind of ecological thinking to be understood and solved. Such new thinking requires a shift in values from growth to conservation, from domination to partnership and from competition to cooperation.

Ultimately, ecological management requires a new worldview and a commitment within every firm to go through radical change in its corporate culture (see chapter 6). This paradigm shift sees the world as integrated rather than a dislocated collection of parts which compete rather than cooperate. Environmental management on the other hand is about a shallow form of environmentalism which accepts a mechanistic paradigm and tends to endorse the ideology of economic growth (albeit often by default). Ecological management has its roots in deep ecology and involves a shift to a holistic worldview. Shallow environmentalism is anthropocentric whereas deep ecology recognises the intrinsic value of all living beings.

Environmental auditing and other environmental management

practices do not question the dominant corporate paradigm (Callenbach *et al.*, 1993). They see the firm as mechanistic, subject to control and they therefore adopt the framework of traditional neo-classical economics. This tends to reinforce the status quo and offers little guidance for a sustainable future. At its worst environmental management based on a paradigm of soft environmentalism becomes a cynical attempt to deceive us. Cosmetic environmental changes are made to improve public relations, increase sales and boost profits. Green marketing campaigns, misleading advertising and inaccurate communications do little to move us to sustainability.

The issue is where do we go if we leave behind the traditional approach to environmental management. A useful way of looking at this issue is to examine exactly what the focus of our audit methodology should be. It is argued here that the dominant approach enshrined in the systems standards which we have discussed above revolves around auditing systems and auditing direct environmental impacts at one point in time. Up to now we have only discussed systems auditing and traditional approaches to environmental auditing. There are other approaches which go beyond these and we should therefore attempt a classification of these different audit approaches.

## ALTERNATIVE ENVIRONMENTAL AUDITING TECHNIQUES

The traditional approach to auditing adopted by many firms has tended not to incorporate ecological impacts which go beyond compliance and directly measurable pollution effects. This is too narrow an approach if our ultimate aim is to move towards sustainability. Table 4.1 outlines five levels of auditing, classified by the central focus of the approach. The most basic approach to auditing is compliance auditing where performance is measured as conformance to legislation, regulation and codes of conduct. Up until the early 1990s the majority of environmental audits were usually little more than compliance audits. Standards such as BS7750 and the eco-management and audit scheme extend the auditing process to systems audits where the focus is on implementing and operating an effective environmental management system which provides for continuous improvement and adherence to self-determined environmental performance targets.

Level 3 in Table 4.1 describes traditional approaches to environmental auditing which take a snap-shot of the environmental performance of a company at one point in time. The main focus is on the direct impact of an organisation, site or process on water, land and the air and therefore concentrates on direct pollution effects, contingency planning and health and safety. BS7750 and the eco-management and audit scheme demand a clear and complete approach to auditing at levels 1 and 2 and some requirements to consider environmental issues at level 3 (although arguably these are rather piecemeal). In addition we should recognise that for these three levels the mode of assessment is essentially static, focusing on direct, easily measurable impacts and conformity to the law and management system in place, all at one particular point in time. Each audit is discrete and repeated periodically in an attempt to provide information to manage improvement. But such a process does not mimic the more dynamic nature of ecological processes which are constantly changing.

Going beyond traditional environmental auditing techniques requires a change in emphasis in a number of ways. At level 4 we ought to introduce the concept of ecological auditing which has three key features. Firstly, the mode of assessment must be dynamic, recognising that ecosystems which change over time are of central importance and that the environment is a highly intricate and interlinked process rather than a fixed resource. A dynamic approach looks at impact well into the future, stressing the cumulative effect of ecological damage and the long term effect some impacts have on ecosystems. It should not be a bounded assessment undertaken at one point in time.

Secondly, there needs to be an increased emphasis put on life cycle assessment as the tool of analysis (see chapter 5). This is because life cycle assessment forces us to track products from cradle to grave and to put greater emphasis on all the impacts associated with raw materials extraction, processing at every stage, distribution, use of the product and disposal. It makes us focus on the indirect as well as direct impact of any activity.

Thirdly, a wider set of ecological issues need to be addressed. We need to move away from the mentality of health-and-safety-type audits where it is human well-being which is paramount, towards valuing all living animals, protecting biodiversity and putting the emphasis on living in harmony with nature. This requires us to move away from short term planning horizons towards more long

Table 4.1 Environmental auditing techniques

| Type of audit | Level 1<br>Compliance auditing | Level 2<br>Systems auditing | Level 3<br>Environmental auditing | Level 4<br>Ecological auditing | Level 5<br>Auditing for sustainability |
|---|---|---|---|---|---|
| Central foci | Legislation<br><br>Regulations<br><br>Voluntary standards<br>Consents and discharge permits | Level 1 plus:<br><br>Environmental management systems<br><br>Self-determined targets and objectives | Levels 1 and 2 plus:<br><br>Direct environmental impact on:<br>water,<br>air and<br>land<br><br>Health and safety<br><br>Protection of employees and the community<br><br>Contingency planning | Levels 1 to 3 plus:<br><br>Intertemporal impact on eco-systems<br><br>Life cycle assessment of products<br><br>Measurement of indirect ecological impacts<br><br>Recognition of need to live in harmony with nature | Levels 1 to 4 plus:<br><br>Equity and equality<br><br>Futurity<br><br>Protection of indigenous populations<br><br>Construction of a social and ethical balance sheet<br><br>Holistic approach |
| Assessment | Static | Static | Static | Dynamic | Dynamic |

term inter-generational holistic planning. In effect environmental auditing is anthropocentric whereas ecological auditing is founded on a recognition of a need to live in harmony with nature.

The distinction between environmental auditing and ecological auditing is further illustrated by comparing definitions of these alternative approaches. According to the International Chamber of Commerce (1989) an environmental audit is:

> a management tool comprising a systematic, documented, periodic and objective evaluation of how well environmental organisation, management and equipment are performing with the aim of helping to safeguard the environment by: (i) facilitating management and control of environmental practices; and (ii) assessing compliance with company policies, which include meeting regulatory requirements.

According to the Elmwood Institute (Callenbach *et al.*, 1993) an ecological audit is:

> an examination and review of a company's operations from the perspective of deep ecology, or the new paradigm. It is motivated by a shift in values within the corporate culture from domination to partnership, from the ideology of economic growth to that of ecological sustainability. It involves a corresponding shift from mechanistic to systemic thinking and accordingly, a new style of management know as systemic management. The result of the ecological audit is an action plan for minimising the company's environmental impact and making all its operations more ecologically sound.

In effect, the distinction between environmental management and ecological management is at the root of the differences between levels three and four. Ecological management and ecological auditing represent a fundamental shift in the dominant paradigm underlying the management of the organisation. This is not the end of the matter however. Going back to our auditing model, there is a fifth level, auditing for sustainability, which firms will have to move towards if we are ever to move to a model of sustainable development. Since this is the central focus of the book we ought therefore to consider this whole area in more detail.

## AUDITING FOR SUSTAINABILITY

The central focus of level 5 auditing is to go back to the key concept of sustainability and audit for sustainability. This is a holistic approach predicated on a clear worldview and an understanding of the need for further 'paradigm shift' in business culture (Commoner, 1990; Welford, 1994b; Wheeler, 1993). Organisations auditing for sustainability should be committed to integrating environmental performance to wider issues of global ecology and make specific reference to the concepts associated with sustainable development. Thus, as a starting point, energy-efficiency should be focused on the need to minimise $NO_x$, $SO_x$ and $CO_2$ emissions and avoid nuclear waste. Waste minimisation, re-use and recycling should be driven by the need to conserve non-renewable resources. Product design should prioritise the use of renewable resources. Sourcing of raw materials should have no negative impacts on global biodiversity, endangered habitats or the rights of indigenous peoples. Overall corporate policies should examine the business impact on both the developed and underdeveloped world, both now and into the future.

The key question relates to the extent to which the environmental management system approach (typified in chapter 3) can actually deliver sustainability. Where such systems are based on a continuous cycle of improvement, sustainability may take a very long time to achieve. Moreover, the auditing process encompassed in the quality-driven environmental management system is dominated by the audit of the system, procedures, documents and management rather than environmental damage. The fact that many firms are embracing management systems such as BS7750 is explained by the fact that they are easily achievable, particularly in organisations where a quality management system is already in place, and they highlight the idea that an organisation is doing something rather than nothing.

The traditional management systems approach stresses the continuous cycle of improvement. Progress continues to take place therefore unless that cycle is interrupted. However, we know from the more mature experience of systems such as ISO9000 (BS5750) that this cycle does indeed sometimes break down. One of the biggest challenges of the whole total quality management approach is to keep up momentum and there are countless examples where that has not been achieved. Common reasons for the breakdown in the continuous cycle range from simple complacency through to alternative competing agendas which push the original objectives down the list of corporate priorities.

There is a contradiction which arises when, as so many firms have done, organisations commit themselves to sustainable development and then opt for an approach which does not necessarily achieve these fundamental aims. One of the key problems that has arisen is that by adopting a quality-driven environmental management system approach, firms believe that they are adopting principles of sustainable development. They seem to be of the view that environmental improvement equates to sustainable development. This is clearly not the case, as a closer look at the sustainable development concept reveals.

What is required is a shift in paradigms towards an acceptance by industry of its ethical and social responsibilities. If that is an insufficient reason for change in a profit driven world then businesses should recognise that it is not only ethical to be environmentally friendly, but with the growth of consumer awareness in the environmental area, it will also be good for sales. Such an approach continues to leave aside the key concepts of futurity and equity however and these are fundamental to an approach which is about sustainability management.

Firms clearly have a role to play in the development of substitutes for non-renewable resources and innovations which reduce waste and use energy more efficiently. They also have a role in processing those materials in a way which brings about environmental improvements. For many products (e.g. cars and washing machines), the major area of environmental damage occurs in their usage. Firms often have the opportunity of reducing this damage at the design stage and when new products are being developed there is a whole new opportunity for considering both the use and disposal of the product. But this all ought to be done in the context of ensuring that operations do not exploit the developing world and its peoples. Moreover, environmental costs ought to be properly accounted, that is, they ought to be measured on a timescale which has not to date been used. The real cost of using non-renewable resources when measured over time therefore approaches infinity since once used they are lost for ever. This is rarely considered.

The majority of firms who are doing anything at all to try to improve their environmental performance have now adopted auditing procedures based on a systems approach. Such an approach may take a business round in circle after circle of incremental improvement but where the starting point for this environmental merry-go-round is fundamentally unsustainable it is unlikely to result in the significant step up in environmental performance which the world needs. The alternative approach is to undertake environmental audits based not on the principles of management systems but on the fundamental principle of sustainable development. That is not to suggest that management systems are not important; they are. But they should be seen as the vehicle which drives environmental improvement and not the measure of success themselves.

Auditing for sustainability requires firms to look at their overall impact on the environment, on equity and on futurity and to construct a social and ethical balance sheet. It challenges firms to prioritise their actions in ecological terms rather than management systems terms. Moreover, it must be recognised that whilst bad systems may worsen environmental degradation, it is not the systems themselves which cause the damage but the products and services for which the system is designed. Rather than auditing systems, therefore, we ought to place more emphasis on auditing products and therefore there is a central emphasis on the need for life cycle assessment (see chapter 5).

However, the barrier to such a development is the very economy–environment nexus which we seem to have created for ourselves over the past few years. That framework is achievable, manageable and has the backing of an all-powerful industry. It is a nexus which fits well into present systems at the company level as well as at the level of the economy. The fact that that comfortable nexus goes only a small way to achieving the fundamental need to audit for sustainability is the flaw in the approach. Such a piece-meal approach may satisfy the demands of the customers of some companies, it may well give companies a good feeling about some of the ethics involved in their activities. It does not go very far in achieving real sustainable development however.

## THE NEED FOR A NEW IDEOLOGY

In earlier chapters of this book we have already suggested that significant evidence exists that management trends which become popular exert a strong influence on the on-going techniques of corporate management. New concepts which are successfully implemented in certain organisations become accepted, become dominant and even when they are inappropriate become the norm (Mintzberg, 1979).

These are precisely the trends which we are seeing in the adoption of the quality-driven approaches to environmental management. It has been argued that this approach is not entirely appropriate to the concept of sustainable development in that it does not go far enough. But this approach is becoming the accepted ideology because it is being adopted by leading firms, espoused by academics and legitimised through standard setters such as the British Standards Institute and the European Union.

Moreover, this trend is further reinforced by benchmarking analysis in industry. As a principle, benchmarking can be valuable but it can also reinforce inappropriate general techniques. It has been argued that current standards are not high, and this in turn gives the impression to imitators in industry that the environmental challenge facing industry is actually quite weak. The reverse is quite true and what is needed therefore is a change in the dominant ideology.

Such a change in ideology is, of course, difficult to achieve because environmental management standards have been set by industry itself. They have been designed to be voluntary and designed so as not to conflict with the ideology associated with profit maximisation in the short to medium term. Arguments such as the ones outlined above, suggesting that industry has not gone far enough, will therefore be treated with derision by many in industry and sidelined. The power which industry has in the current economic system is therefore a barrier to further development of the concepts of sustainable development. Thus the only way to bring about a change in this suboptimal dominant ideology is to challenge the very basis of that power. Without a fundamental revolution in the way we organise our society, such a challenge can only come about through a legislative process.

## THE LEGISLATIVE FRAMEWORK

The premise taken here is that there is a need for tougher legislation which would include requirements on businesses to measure their environmental impacts widely defined. Moreover there is a need for national legislation which not only protects domestic economies but also those of developing countries. Such an approach represents a radical shift in the foundations of industrial policy and firms will, of course, complain that the real requirements for sustainable development will impose severe costs and competitive disadvantage on them. They will not, however, disagree on the need to create the ubiquitous 'level playing field' and the clear implication of this is that industry itself should have a vested interest and should be campaigning for a tougher legislative stance on the part of governments across the whole world. Such a campaign should be based on making sure that the whole of industry faces a common set of minimum standards. The problem associated with alternative voluntary approaches is that some firms can create a cost advantage for themselves simply by not adopting those voluntary codes, which further weakens adherence in the whole industry.

There is a need to develop a new set of environmental standards which take us beyond the piecemeal approach identified in the previous chapter. Part of those new standards should insist on the public disclosure of environmental information about their performance, verified by third parties. Compulsory environmental auditing and public reporting of audit results should be introduced in those industries identified as having particular negative environmental impacts. Moreover, the standards must be common across countries and mandatory and must be based on the three fundamental principles of sustainable development, not the environment in isolation.

There will be arguments which will suggest that such common standards may be achievable at the level of the individual nation state, or even across national groupings such as the European Union. There will be those who will argue that companies or even whole countries operating in the less developed world will simply escape these minimum standards. We must recognise though that such standards are fundamental to the continuance of life on the planet and as such are fundamentally superior to the interests of international trade. For companies and countries not willing to comply with environmental standards, protectionist measures against them are therefore justified.

## IMPLEMENTING AN APPROPRIATE SYSTEMIC APPROACH

In this chapter we have stressed the need for a systemic approach but criticised the traditional approach which audits the environmental management system. There is not a contradiction here since we are arguing that the environmental management system must be the vehicle for change but is not the measure of change as implied by standards such as BS7750. To move towards sustainability requires us to implement a systemic approach but not to be bounded by traditional management thinking, structures and paradigms. Part of the systemic approach is to put a new emphasis on creativity.

Putting an effective environmental management system or indeed any management system in place in an organisation is not easy, is time consuming and as a process itself will never end because there will always be improvements which can be made. An intellectual understanding of environmental and of ecological issues provides the basis of the environmental management system but this has to be translated into commitment, policies, organisation, plans and actions for environmental improvement. The commitment to the system needs to be kept up and members of the organisation need to have the importance of management system reinforced periodically. Without this on-going commitment the whole initiative will eventually be marginalised and disappear and as with any change programme the whole workforce needs to realise that the strategy is a continual process. There is therefore a key on-going need for training and help with the implementation process and development of the environmental management system over time. Much of this implies a change in corporate culture but it should be remembered that organisations which try to change their environmental culture, without effectively communicating their objectives and reasons to everyone involved in that organisation, will not succeed.

It is often a good idea to identify a management team who will drive the initiative and coordinate the strategies. That team will have to ensure that the implementation of the system remains high on the agenda. Having a clear target to aim for will often help to focus efforts and therefore the ultimate aim of attaining accreditation with a standard such as BS7750 can act as a very positive impetus as the first step to a sustainable organisation. We have already noted however that the systemic approach cannot be implemented from above but must be evolved with the commitment and support of the entire workforce. This will often require a new style of leadership based around systemic management. The Elmwood Institute (Callenbach *et al.*, 1993) advocates leadership based around four key points:

1 Systemically oriented managers do not see themselves as dominators and controllers within the company, but rather as 'cultivators' or 'catalysts'. Being aware of the nature of the company as a living system, they give 'impulses' rather than instructions.

2 Systemic managers learn how to live with uncertainty. They act within a social system which they cannot fully comprehend and whose reactions and events they will never predict with certainty, let alone control. This does not relieve them, however, from the responsibility for providing guidance to the organisation.

3 The view of the stability and flexibility of a social system as a consequence of its dynamic balance suggests a corresponding strategy of conflict resolution. In every company, as in society as a whole, conflicts and contradictions will invariably appear that cannot be simply resolved in favour of one or the other side. Thus we need stability and change, order and freedom, tradition and innovation, planning and laissez-faire.

4 A systemically oriented manager knows that the contradictions within the company are signs of its variety and vitality, and thus contribute to the system's viability. Without conflicts there can be little development. A systemic manager will therefore try to take into account both sides of a contradiction, knowing that both will be important depending on context. He or she will try to solve inevitable conflicts not by means of rigid decisions but rather through balancing both sides.

The systemic approach demands that the implementation of any system is also done in a systemic way. Welford and Gouldson (1993) lay out ten stages central to the implementation of a traditional environmental management system. Essentially this involves senior management undertaking and developing the following ideas:

1 Understand the environmental challenge in relation to its

global, national and local contexts and particularly in relation to your own organisation.

2 Be committed to environmental improvement and communicate that commitment to the whole workforce and, indeed, to all stakeholders and move environmental issues up the environmental agenda.

3 Establish an environmental policy and any associated objectives and publish them widely. Consider the appointment of a person with a brief for environmental initiatives who will be responsible to the chief executive.

4 Assess and measure the extent of environmental damage within the organisation, in other words undertake an initial environmental review and subsequent, regular environmental audits.

5 Organise and structure the Environmental Management System so that it is efficient, effective and can be understood by the workforce. Identify any gaps which emerge in the system and take steps to rectify them.

6 Decide on the organisation's environmental priorities and structure plans to improve environmental performance.

7 Introduce training in order to make all members of the organisation aware of relevant environmental issues, to help them understand the plans and to facilitate the environmental management system.

8 Carefully introduce and continually develop your environmental management system in order to achieve environmental improvement. Make sure that the system is properly understood and communicated to all relevant parties.

9 Record achievements and impediments to improvement and act on them ensuring that gaps are plugged.

10 Do it all again ensuring that the message is reinforced and that systems and environmental performance are continually improved.

Following these ten stages can, but will not necessarily, lead to a successful environmental management system. Neither should they imply a mechanistic or narrow technologically based approach which looks only at one issue at a time. Such an approach will be hampered by the limitations of current scientific knowledge, competing demands on capital expenditure and management time, conflicts between competing organisational objectives and the power of technical expertise in decision making. What is needed is a complete and holistic approach which implies that an evolution-ary, integrated and proactive approach needs to be taken to environmental issues. Indeed, if we are to stress the need to move towards sustainability then that approach must integrate social and ethical considerations alongside environmental ones. Moreover, the system must be capable of considering much longer time horizons than is common in most businesses.

The precise order of the ten stages identified may be changed to suit the particular operation or organisation but it should be stressed that they are not one-off or discrete tasks. They have to be approached in an integrated way and continuously revisited. However, the ten stages do provide the building blocks of the system and provide a structured path to be followed and repeated. It cannot be stressed too much that a culture or philosophy which creates corporate commitment to sustainable development needs to be developed.

The ten-point plan identified above is firmly placed within the context of environmental management, however, and we have argued in this chapter that we need to move on to ecological management and sustainability management. Underlying this ten-point strategy there is therefore a need to adopt an overall approach encompassing the following requirements for achieving sustainability:

1 Recognise the central importance of ecological improvement, of business ethics and of sustainable development and record this in a clear policy statement.
2 Adopt a new philosophy towards the organisation's operations which sees environmental damage, the maintenance of unequal and inequitable trading relationships and short-termism as unacceptable.
3 Ensure that ecological and ethical improvement is endogenous to all systems and processes and develop teams to improve those processes in a cooperative way.
4 When assessing production possibilities, measure total costs, not just internalised private costs and identify and cost potential environmental problems, and when considering products undertake full life cycle assessments of their impacts.
5 Make it clear that management is committed to a sustainable future and sees that as a key element of corporate performance.
6 Institute modern methods of systemic management which will

promote motivation, participatory arrangements, improved information and communication flows and adequate and high quality training and retraining.

7 Measure all ecological impacts of all activities of the firm in a dynamic way recognising the importance of ecosystems and the need to protect nature.

8 Take a holistic view of the operation of the business now and into the future.

9 Value the workforce, involve them in process development, encourage them to establish their own environmental, ethical and social goals and reward them accordingly.

10 Audit for sustainability and record and act on impediments to sustainable development.

Where environmental management systems accredited to BS7750 or the eco-management and audit scheme already exist in an organisation these can be built on to embrace the ecological management and sustainability as well. We must however recognise that sustainable organisations require a systemic and holistic approach but that the systemic approach common in environmental management systems standards falls far short of dealing with the central issues within sustainable development. It is also important to stress the role of every person in the organisation and the need to adopt a participatory style of management where the workforce is involved and valued and not treated as a discrete factor of production. Creativity will often be an important tool in developing the sorts of strategies which we need.

## CONCLUSION

It is no longer sufficient to see environmental strategy as an add-on to other corporate policies. Environmental improvement and the avoidance of accidental damage needs to be firmly embedded at all levels of the organisation. Central here is a need for a proactive stance and an evolutionary approach to the improvement of environmental performance. This can be achieved by adopting the type of environmental management system outlined here. Moreover, environmental management is no longer an option. Increased legislation, the European eco-management and audit scheme, consumer pressure and pressure on suppliers from organisations with their own environmental policies mean that the establishment of environmental management systems cannot be seen simply as a 'competitive edge', they will in time become a means of survival.

However, we have identified the need to go even further than this and fully integrate all the components of sustainable development into a new way of doing business. Environmental management and its associated systems standards only go part of the way to creating a sustainable future. This chapter is not suggesting that current environmental management practice is bad or that innovations such as the eco-management and auditing scheme and BS7750 are a waste of time. They do provide principles which all firms should work towards. The issue is whether they go far enough. The eco-management and audit scheme is clearly superior to BS7750 because of its requirement for verification and reporting but it is still overtly management-system driven. The key concept of sustainable development requires a new approach to business and we have seen little evidence of a radical paradigm shift either in the eco-management and auditing or the BS7750 standards. Current approaches are suboptimal and inappropriate but they are still likely to be adopted widely because they will become part of a dominant ideology. A responsible and proactive approach to the environment requires new and radical approaches to doing business. This will include the need for increasing not decreasing legislation which industry itself should be campaigning for.

Rethinking business strategy along the lines of sustainable development does require a change in corporate cultures and it therefore opens up new opportunities to reassess other aspects of business. Issues that need also to be addressed in line with environmental demands include worker participation, democracy in the workplace, the treatment of women and minority groups, animal testing, public accountability, and the impact on the Third World and indigenous populations. Indeed, these issues should not be seen as separate entities but as part of a new overall strategy for doing business ethically and holistically. Moreover, the very power which endorses a piecemeal approach to environmental improvement is the same power which continues to deny rights to workers and to the less developed countries. The same system which exploits the natural environment also exploits women, ethnic minorities, indigenous populations, people with different sexual orientations and other minority groups. Being forced to deal with these issues will necessarily challenge the very foundations of the system which we too often seen as immovable and will therefore be opposed by vested interests. Nevertheless, such ideas are achievable and indeed fundamental to the very existence of the planet on which we live.

Ultimately, systems and structures will have to change and we will need to find new ways of doing business which protect the whole range of global diversity. That will demand culture change at every level of organisation in the world. To suggest that this is not achievable cannot be true. The rigid systems of market-driven and profit-centred capitalism and of output-orientated state planning, which have been largely responsible for environmental degradation throughout the world are both flawed. In the history of the world, or just of humankind, such systems have not existed for very long and something else will follow in time. In the shorter term, however, culture change can be achieved at the level of the firm. But before going on to deal with the issue of culture change, in detail, in chapter 6, we will return to the central concept and technique of life cycle assessment identified in this chapter as so important.

# 5

LIFE CYCLE ASSESSMENT

## INTRODUCTION

The principles of life cycle assessment are not new. In the 1970s, fuel cycle studies were common amongst very high energy users who wanted to minimise energy consumption. Life cycle costing techniques have also been used by some management accountants in trying to build up a clearer picture of overhead cost allocation. Only in the past few years, however, has life cycle assessment really spread to become a tool which identifies the activities that are involved in the whole life of a product. This profile can then be used in the assessment of environmental burdens.

Life cycle assessment (LCA) is about taking a cradle-to-grave approach. In other words it is about an analysis covering every stage and every significant environmental impact of a product from the extraction and use of raw materials through to the eventual disposal of the components of the product and their decomposition back to the elements. However, in trying to stress the complete life cycle of the product we might consider using the terms from conception to resurrection and for practical purposes of business strategy we should stress that it is about design to recycling. We will see that it is at the design stage where much can be done to improve a product's overall environmental performance.

Life cycle assessment has sometimes been seen as a controversial field of study. Fundamentally it is a tool to be used to shed light on the product's environmental impact at every stage from extraction to disposal. The detailed LCA research study may, for example, include mining, forestry techniques, energy and water use, air and water pollution, solid and hazardous waste production, damage occurring during the use of the product (including an assessment of possible misuse) and the repair, re-use, recycleability and disposal of a product. LCA can be used to compare the environmental impacts of similar products. For example, it might be used to assess the environmental impact of a polystyrene cup versus a paper cup versus a conventional pottery cup. Starting from the acquisition of the raw material and the effects of the manufacturing processes, and working throughout the product life cycle from manufacture to disposal (including an evaluation of the energy and water used in washing the pottery alternative), the sum of net effects can be evaluated, compared and a decision taken about the option which causes least damage.

The LCA process is necessarily quite complex and detailed. It requires the active cooperation of suppliers, and collaboration is a prerequisite for progress. However, since life cycle assessment has been taken seriously by businesses, there is increasing concern that LCA may become a non-ecological activity. For example, it is clearly in the interest of suppliers of bulk commodities to draw the boundaries of LCA quite tightly in order to focus attention on those factors which are most easily controlled: wastes, polluting emissions and energy consumption. However, a full ecological consideration of product life cycles also has to take into account the impact of raw material procurement on biodiversity, endangered habitats, human and animal rights and non-renewable resources. Ignoring these issues may be convenient (especially to the agrochemical, petrochemical, chemical and mining industries), but it is not tolerable from an ecological perspective (Wheeler, 1993a).

## THE ADVANTAGES OF LIFE CYCLE ASSESSMENT

Life cycle assessment brings with it a number of advantages often overlooked by traditional environmental auditing methodologies. The concentration on the product, rather than the system, facilitates direct measurement of environmental impact. Being directly linked to products also means that environmental strategy can be linked into the marketing system and therefore marketing and environmental strategy become intertwined (see chapter 7). LCA also widens the environmental analysis beyond management systems and site-specific production attributes which can so easily hide environmental damage up or down the supply chain. The product-specific approach also aids environmental communication because of the clear link between LCA and eco-labelling.

A concentration on products also allows us to track the inputs into the production process, allows us to track the sources of those inputs and therefore allows us to say something about possible impacts on underdeveloped countries and the concepts of equity and futurity. It is therefore a tool which can more directly measure progress towards sustainable development. Moreover, tracking the life-cycle of the product forward enables us to say much more about environmental damage than we can in a traditional assessment of processes. Again, it fundamentally places the concept of futurity within our overall measurement of performance.

The process of life cycle assessment puts more emphasis on the role of design and re-design. It is often accepted that 80 to 90 per cent of the total life cycle costs associated with a product are committed by the final design of the product before production or construction actually begins (Fabrycky and Blanchard, 1991; Gatenby and Foo, 1990). Similarly waste resulting from the product creation, use and disposal are largely determined by original design. To date, this has not been the central focus of the design phase, however, nor have designers commonly thought about futurity and equity implications of the products which they are developing. However, the LCA and auditing for sustainability approaches raise these issues and push them to the forefront of the design task. Traditional auditing methodologies perform no such function.

The main application of LCA should therefore be as an internal management tool to assist in the minimisation of product environmental impact. LCA provides an analytical framework through which this can be achieved. As such it should be incorporated into all environmental strategies and the management systems which seek to improve environmental performance.

Life cycle assessment is however, to date, a very underdeveloped area in terms of research and the development of methodologies. For this reason it has not been taken up by that many organisations. It is useful at this stage to highlight one of the key problems with the LCA approach which has dogged its inception. The problem concerns how impractical LCA can be if it is unbounded. In a far-reaching life cycle assessment absolutely everything connected with a particular product would have to be measured and all measurements and impacts would have to be assessed according to an unlimited time horizon. Whilst this is perhaps desirable in measures associated with sustainability, it is nonetheless impossible. Unless bounds are placed on the assessment, the inventory of impacts grows exponentially. There is therefore a fundamental need to put boundaries in place and this will involve fundamental decisions being made. Such decisions are not easy when our ultimate aim is measurement with respect to the environment, to equity and to futurity. This is therefore an area where we need some fundamental research and debate.

LCA aims to assess and therefore help producers to minimise the environmental impact of a product at all stages in its life. As an internal management tool for the company, the application of LCA is a way of clearly establishing the impact of a product throughout its life and hence a way of identifying key areas for attention. Within the firm, whether this is carried out in an exact, objective or quantitative way is not of fundamental importance. The benefits of LCA accrue through the focusing of managerial minds on all aspects of the product's environmental profile. The undertaking of this process will automatically aid future decision making to better incorporate the environmental dimension and therefore to lessen impact.

The EU eco-labelling scheme is based on the application of LCA. It aims to assess and recognise best practice in minimising overall product impact and to communicate these achievements to potential customers. It is therefore necessary to compare and rank the environmental impact of a number of different products and to award the label to the best environmental performers. Once the label becomes widely adopted it could provide the necessary information on product environmental impact to all those who are interested and negate the need for supplier questionnaires. To do this effectively the process of LCA must be developed to provide an objective and widely accepted framework though which the environmental impact of similar products can be measured and compared. However, the process of LCA is as yet far from being an exact and objective science.

## THE LCA PROCESS

The aim of LCA is to highlight those particular areas in the environmental profile of a product where producers or vendors should focus their response in order to minimise their environmental impact. In many cases such a response will be through the redesign of the product. Should the major area of environmental impact be during use, for example, with the case of washing machines, then efforts to reduce the impact of the good should centre on providing the consumer with better knowledge and advice on how to use the product, and redesigning the product so that its environmental impact during use is reduced. Alternatively, if the major area of environmental impact occurs as a result of the use of non-renewable resources then alternative sources should be sought, and again the product might well undergo some redesign to reduce or eliminate the dependence on scarce resources. In all cases, those aspects of the product which generate significant environmental impact should be revised.

In practical terms, LCA provides a systematic framework through which the constituents of the product and their environmental impacts which are selected for study can be analysed and the potential for impact reduction assessed. In effect, life cycle assessment is an information gathering exercise. It is fundamental to new product development and should be a regular tool of analysis whenever a product is redesigned. LCA attempts to provide information on all facets of a product's environmental performance and the results of the assessment must be incorporated into the overall environmental management strategy of the firm. As process and product design are inextricably linked, the importance of an integrated approach which aims to minimise the overall environmental impact of a company cannot be over-emphasised.

The life cycle assessment itself involves a number of stages. These are:

1 The identification of areas of environmental impact in order to enable further assessment.
2 The quantification of energy and material inputs, emissions and waste outputs and any other potential area of environmental damage within the areas identified in 1.
3 An assessment of the environmental impact and impact mechanisms of the areas identified in 2.
4 The establishment of options and strategies for improving each stage of the life cycle of the product.

The strength of the LCA lies in the systematic collection and collation of quantitative data which should establish the extent of any environmental impact and its scope for improvement. Simply going through the LCA process will focus attention on issues which can so easily be ignored and not considered. The process will confirm or challenge any assumptions and pre-conceptions made and it will facilitate a greater understanding of the ecological impacts involved.

There are of course difficulties in the LCA process. One controversy relating to LCA arises when it attempts to quantify and rank a range of different environmental impacts. For example, LCAs undertaken for washing machines have established that without any doubt the most considerable environmental impacts for all washing machines are in their consumption of energy and water during their use (Hemming, 1992). Should one particular washing machine use less water and energy than a competitor, it is clear that its environmental impact is the lower of the two. However, should one be more energy efficient and thus make a lower contribution to global warming whilst a second uses less water and detergent and thus has a lower impact on water consumption and pollution, then objectively establishing which has the lower impact becomes very difficult. With a product significantly more complex than a washing machine (e.g. a car) many argue that the LCA process and any comparisons between products using this process would be impractical. Quite simply, the extraordinary range of raw materials and components used in modern products and the infinite range of interactions with different ecosystems which will occur when emissions are released into the environment, means that quantitatively assessing and ranking the environmental impact of many products with many different impacts becomes virtually impossible.

The potential scope of an LCA is enormous if we were to consider absolutely every environmental impact of the product and all the knock-on effects caused by direct impact on the environment. Impacts which have little or no effect on the environment have to be ignored and there must be some limit to the examination of knock-on effects. It is clear therefore that before beginning the process of LCA, it is important to decide upon the scope and objectives of the exercise and to consider what constitutes a significant environmental impact. It is necessary to set the boundaries of the LCA to manageable limits. Current LCA methodology selects those facets of the process which are likely to provide the most relevant information, for instance in highlighting any inputs which are especially damaging or any stages of procurement, distribution, processing, use or disposal which can be readily improved. For internal use, the scope of LCA may be very selective or partial depending on the objectives to be achieved. However, for external use where comparative measures of total environmental impact are needed, the LCA must be much more detailed and comprehensive.

There are four generally accepted stages in the LCA methodology:

1 Inventory: the definition of the inventory involves gathering quantifiable data relating to the material and energy inputs into a product across its whole life cycle and any associated emissions, discharges and wastes. This should relate to all stages of the product life cycle from extraction and cultivation, procurement, processing, manufacture, packaging, distribution, use, disposal and decomposition. Resources used and emissions generated should be measured per unit of output produced. Although this stage may demand extensive research, particularly for companies which use a large number of inputs or operate along lengthy supply chains, it is relatively straightforward.

2 Impact analysis: impact analysis considers how the inventory may affect the environment and it is therefore much less straightforward than the definition of the inventory. It involves establishing the environmental impact of each of the areas documented under the inventory. This may be extremely complicated because, in many cases, the impact of an emission will depend upon the nature of the emission, the environment into which it is emitted and the interaction of a number of characteristics. The analysis should cover ecological damage, human and animal health, habitat modification and lifestyle changes as a minimum. The boundaries of this stage of LCA will therefore be defined by the depth of analysis which is deemed appropriate, necessary and possible.

3 Impact assessment: once the scope and level of environmental impact has been established, some assessment or measurement of this impact is needed. Impact assessment is often broken down into three distinct phases:

- Classification, which involves grouping the data in an inventory table into a number of impact categories (e.g. human health, natural resources, ecological impact, etc.).
- Characterisation – this phase involves the quantification, aggregation and analysis of impact data within the agreed

105

impact categories. This leads to a number of impact profiles consisting of impact descriptions and associated measures.

- Valuation – this phase involves the weighting of the different impact categories so that they can be compared. Impacts can be established both quantitatively and qualitatively. Quantitative impact assessment develops a list of the amounts of emissions and some measurement of their impact. In many cases, this is as much factual assessment as is possible in the absence of an element of subjectivity. However, an LCA to this point can provide an internal benchmark against which to compare future performance and is therefore of considerable use.

4 Improvement: the final stage of LCA represents feedback for improving the environmental profile of the product. In effect, the improvement stage demonstrates where the environmental profile of the product ought to be altered through redesign of the product and its manufacturing process. A formal and systematic appraisal of the product's environmental impact will often reveal areas where relatively simple fine tuning will reduce environmental impact. The improvement stage will assess the technically and economically feasible options available at all stages of the product's life to improve the environmental impact of the good.

The LCA process is therefore quite intricate and requires considerable analytical skills. There is, of course, a real resource cost to the LCA process itself. In many cases, however, the scope of the study may not necessitate such a comprehensive LCA and the process of LCA might be simplified in a number of ways. Different components of the study can be collated in relation to separate impacts, for instance all those areas where solid waste is generated, energy is consumed and so on. This will reduce the number of variants and simplify the process considerably. For some commonly used inputs such as energy and some raw materials, databases of environmental impact are being established in order to provide common LCA measures. These databases can offer standardised impact assessments for a range of energy and material inputs.

As experience of LCA progresses, skills can be built up and levels of subjectivity will be reduced. As LCA becomes more widely applied, the availability of widely accepted data will increase and hence the process will be simplified. The external application of LCA, although considerably more complex, is therefore set to increase as environmental credentials need to become more transparent.

## CONDUCTING THE LIFE CYCLE ASSESSMENT

In order to demonstrate some of the issues in conducting a life cycle assessment let us examine the process applied to a simple product. Hindle and Payne (1991) examine the case of a cricket ball which can be considered in terms of two different fabrication methods. One type of ball has a real leather outer and the other is made from synthetic leather. The ball is made from the following materials: skinned outer, cork inner, dyes, lace and varnish. Each of the components is considered as coming from a particular source (e.g. leather from cattle and cork from trees). However, this example does not consider wider effects such as the impact of felling the cork trees in the first instance. This in effect is establishing a boundary even though its choice is somewhat arbitrary.

The transformation process of manufacture into a product requires energy and produces waste and pollutants. The leather ball must also be maintained in a controlled environment during storage and this will involve more energy. After considering the impact of use, we must consider how the ball will be disposed of or whether there are re-use or recycling opportunities.

We have identified that at the design stage there is much scope for considering a full life cycle impact. Therefore let us now consider how the impact of the ball will change if we replace the outer layer of leather with a synthetic substitute. The new synthetic material requires the use of a non-renewable petroleum source as an input rather than the cattle hide. The issue here therefore is to consider whether the use of a non-renewable resource and the energy used in its processing is better or worse than the impact of using hide from a cow (which is probably being used predominantly for food) and the associated energy, water and chemical impacts of the tanning process. Assuming that the strict storage requirements to maintain leather do not exist for the synthetic alternative, we might consider reduced impacts in this area. Further let us assume that the impacts of distribution are roughly identical and that any impact from use is negligible. The only other key difference therefore will be in end use of the ball where the outer layer of the synthetic version may be recycleable.

The approach taken to this sort of LCA is summarised in Figure 5.1 which illustrates the life cycle impact of each type of ball. In effect this provides us with a basic inventory. The task is to establish the environmental impact of each of the areas identified in the figure by measurement of energy usage, waste, pollution and other significant environmental impacts. Based on this analysis there should be two outcomes. Firstly an improvement analysis for each type of ball should point towards improvements which can be achieved in the life cycle through redesign or the implementation of new operations. Secondly, some assessment may be made as to which alternative is environmentally superior. However, ultimately this will be based on judgement because some of the environmental impacts may not be strictly comparable. Moreover, some assessment of fitness for use and performance during use will form part of the final decision.

## PROBLEMS WITH LCA

We have already identified the fact that LCA can be difficult and that outcomes will be very dependent on the scope and depth of analysis to be applied to the situation. On top of this we must be aware that when used as a tool of assessment this methodology will introduce other problems because of the judgement and subjectivity which is introduced into an otherwise objective exercise. Let us consider some of these problems in more depth.

### Problem 1: parameters

A fundamental problem occurs at the outset of the environmental inventory which is related to deciding how far-reaching the assessment should be. If we consider paper production for example, should we consider the type of saw used for tree felling? An even deeper assessment might consider where the petrol comes from to drive a chain saw, who is the most efficient petrol producer, where the nuts and bolts came from for the saw and what emissions are generated during its use. There is therefore a need to define appropriate levels of investigation and this can be defined in terms of primary, secondary and tertiary levels of analysis. These boundaries set the cut-off points for analysis and must be agreed before any inventory is finally compiled.

In our example we might consider the sources of wood used in

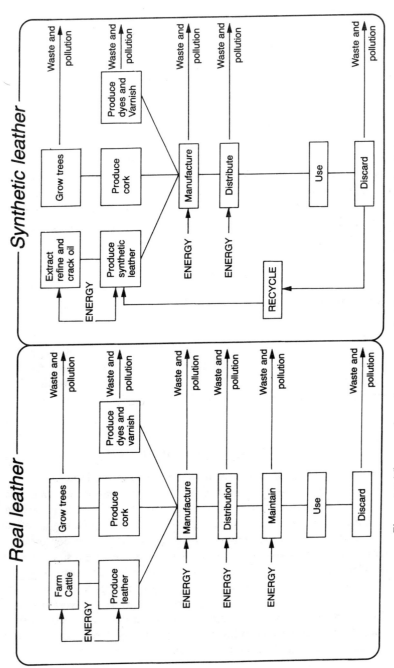

*Figure 5.1* The manufacturing processes for the real and synthetic leather ball

paper production to be at the primary level along with issues of distribution, processing, use and disposal. The environmental impact of the chain saw itself might be considered at the secondary level and the production of the chain saw itself as a tertiary level issue. The decision then relates to how much of the impact at the secondary and tertiary levels is considered in the life cycle assessment.

### Problem 2: comparison of data

Data for energy can be expressed in joules, mass of physical waste can be measured in kilogrammes and air pollution in terms of parts per million. A problem arises when the environmental impact of these different measures are to be compared in terms of their impact on the environment. For example, is one extra part per million of an air pollutant more or less damaging than an extra kilogramme of a water-borne waste, given the same toxic level? Any such comparison would seem to depend on a significant degree of subjectivity because it is impossible to combine all the inventory data into a single number that gives a weighting to all the possible unknowns.

The same sorts of issues are relevant to the comparison of end products. To what extent is it really possible to compare two different technologies which perform the same task for example? Consider the electric kettle versus a gas kettle. Where would we begin to make the sorts of comparisons necessary to begin to form some sort of judgement?

### Problem 3: combination of issues

Problem 2 introduced the idea that disposal to ground may or may not be more damaging than disposal to air or sea but we cannot really tell without a thorough investigation of the impacts on ecosystems in the short and long term. Moreover, our one kilogramme of waste may not cause much damage alone but when combined with other wastes and discharges it may react to cause a significant problem into the future. Thus any comparison of wastes must consider timescales, the combined impact of other polluters' activities and must, in turn, value different kinds of ecosystems in different ways. Thus any comparison of different effects must consider the direct and indirect impacts of a pollutant and might involve some scenario planning and analysis.

110

## Problem 4: disposal and decomposition

A major problem in our modern consumerist age is that when some products have been used up it is economically and (arguably) environmentally more efficient to throw them away rather than to use up the energy and other resources which might be needed in recycling them. However, what is rarely considered in this sort of analysis is the damage done to the environment in the longer term. If products are sent to landfill sites then we evaluate the disposal in terms of the cost of landfill and the loss of resources. We rarely consider the impact of decomposition, of landfill leakage which will in part be caused by our product and the effect of land-use change. Extending our analysis beyond disposal to include decomposition effects is extremely difficult of course.

## Problem 5: assignable cause

The whole process of life cycle analysis and the quantification of environmental damage assumes that impact occurring as a result of the product belong to that product and should be assessed and costed accordingly. This assumes that there are clearly identifiable and assignable property rights. However, since property rights do not exist for much of the environment, then exact quantification of environmental damage is subjective and quantitative assessment must be based on judgements. Moreover where pollution is caused by a combination of impacts from two or more different products, which should be assigned that damage? It might be that one product's impact is negligible until mixed with the other. Both owners of the product are likely to want to assign the damage to the other in those cases.

These five problems need to be addressed at the planning stage of any life cycle assessment. They will sometimes be difficult to reconcile but that does not make the LCA process ineffective or useless. In many cases a change in attitude or business practices towards ecological management holds the answer to the problem. In terms of the problem over assignable cause, the acceptance of strict liability would seem to provide an answer here. In terms of disposability, if we imposed the true cost of disposal and decomposition into the price of the goods, less may be bought. Moreover, if we put more emphasis on designing products which were worth repairing and re-using then the issue of disposal is reduced. This, in turn, is about producing goods which are of high quality.

## WIDENING THE INVENTORY AND IMPACT ANALYSIS

We have suggested in previous chapters that we must now move beyond the realms of traditional approaches of environmental management towards techniques consistent with ecological management and the attainment of sustainable development. The issues which we identified in chapter 4 can also be mirrored in terms of life cycle assessment and the issues which are seen as relevant within the exercise. Because LCA puts the emphasis on the product it is much more feasible to track ecological impacts (widely defined) along the whole life of the product.

If we are ever to reach the aims of sustainable development we will have to widen our definition of environmental or ecological impacts and therefore, when we conduct a life cycle assessment our inventory must include wider issues associated with sustainability. Although this makes the process more complex we ought, for example, to include in our inventory issues such as animal testing, an appropriate respect for all living things and their habitats, biodiversity and species preservation, human health, the rights of indigenous populations to lead traditional lives if they so wish, workers' rights and industrial democracy, the rights of women and minority groups and impacts on the Third World. Life cycle assessment provides us with a tool to take a wider holistic approach and it should be central to our strategies for ecological management and sustainability.

## CONCLUSION

Life cycle assessment is an under-used, under-researched and under-rated tool of analysis. By forcing us to track a particular product (or service) from cradle to grave it forces us to widen our environmental dimensions. It is central to approaches which go beyond traditional environmental management techniques and in its purest form it will begin to evaluate wider ecological impacts and other issues consistent with the attainment of sustainability. However, in its most narrow form LCA can be used to mislead an already sceptical audience and therefore we need carefully to establish the scope and boundaries of any analysis.

Central to the outcomes of the LCA is the improvement analysis which enables us to redesign products to improve their environmental characteristics at all stages of the life cycle. Although we have identified many problems in reaching this stage, further research in LCA techniques and the construction of databases detailing the environmental impacts of common processes, components and substances will begin to make fuller life cycle assessments more feasible. There will always be problems with assigning the cause of environmental problems to particular products and particular producers because of the range of processes and impacts which have diverse knock-on effects. However, a more responsible attitude to the environment based on the precautionary principle will begin to mitigate this problem as well. As with most management tools, LCA must be used effectively, there must be commitment to correcting the deficiencies which the analysis turns up and there must be a continuous process of improvement. Such an approach will need to be ethical and take an ever wider view of the definition of the environment and sustainability.

# 6

# CULTURE CHANGE[1]

## INTRODUCTION

The activities, strategies and techniques outlined in the previous five chapters are all central to moving towards a sustainable model of the business enterprise. What binds much of this together is the recognition of the need for a vehicle to put creative, imaginative and, at times, radical solutions in place. That vehicle is a culture change programme centred on the re-evaluation of global, organisational and individual values.

Corporate culture may be defined as a cohesion of ideas, values, norms and modes of conduct, which have been accepted and adopted by a company. That culture then constitutes a distinctive character of the organisation. The challenge facing the modern business is therefore how it can redefine and change its corporate culture in such a way as to be consistent with the concept of sustainable development.

Culture change within the organisation will require everybody within that organisation to reconsider their own roles, perceptions and values. Senior management will have to take the lead. As a start Callenbach *et al.* (1993) suggest that top managers ask themselves the following questions:

- Am I really concerned about the state of the world, or will I merely act to give myself a better image or boost my ego?
- Do I really understand the key ideas of ecology, or do I merely repeat a few buzzwords?
- Do I myself live in an ecologically conscious way, or is there a discrepancy between my words and acts?

[1]This chapter was written with David Jones

114

- To what extent are the principles of systemic management part of our corporate culture?

It will also be necessary to consider the very business which the firm undertakes and the nature of the industry in which it is involved. For example one ought to consider whether the products or services of the industry are fundamentally destructive to the world's stock of non-renewable resources, or result in significant pollution and contamination. This naturally leads on to a consideration of what changes could make the industry less ecologically damaging. However, it is at the level of the firm that this chapter concentrates. There is a need to consider the sustainability of the company and to redefine corporate goals to make them compatible with a sustainable future.

## NEW PERCEPTIONS AND NEW VALUES

The concept of sustainable development, which goes far beyond incremental environmental improvement, cannot be successfully achieved at the level of the firm through prescriptive strategies involving traditional environmental management techniques (with an emphasis on management systems) alone. It is, however, through developing real commitment within all individuals and by emancipating the worker, encouraging him or her to play a full role within the workplace, that we can begin to make the more radical shift towards a sustainable economic model. But without ensuring an individual's understanding and real commitment to sustainable development, each individual's potential contribution will be overlooked in favour of a more traditional management system and piecemeal approach to the problem. A prime example of this inadequate approach is that enshrined within total quality management (TQM) which through total quality environmental management (TQEM) is considered by some to be the most proactive method of achieving sustainable development.

In previous chapters we have argued that the empowerment of workers and the introduction of participatory arrangements within industry are major steps forward in defining a workable model of sustainable development. However, all too often the extent of this empowerment is management-controlled and individual participation in decision making is limited and thereby stifled. Moreover, corporate vision and corporate culture is often narrowly linked to specific products, markets and modes of operation. Any attempt at culture change in a traditional sense is ultimately dependent upon the manager being able to persuade, to insist or to cajole others into accepting (or sharing) the managerial goal or vision (Plant, 1987). At worst, this approach, which is implicit within TQM, is a deliberate attempt to exert and retain managerial hegemony. In other words, it is an approach where workers have to recognise and then fall into line with what is considered legitimate to change by senior management. Therefore, there is a tendency to introduce innately restrictive measurements throughout the business process, to produce a conveyor belt of incremental targets for the workforce. Another problem with the traditional approach is that an organisation may find that its espoused corporate culture based on a particular definition of sustainable development or environmental improvement has not got the backing of its workforce because each individual is not thinking laterally about real change, but thinking solely of improving the management system (Dodge *et al.*, 1993).

Sustainable development can be achieved only through a means of decision making which is much more democratic, egalitarian, creative and participative than TQM. Considerable research has shown that when regulation is through choice (i.e. is self-determined) people are not only more intrinsically motivated but they are more creative, display greater cognitive flexibility and conceptual understanding, have a more positive emotional tone, are healthier, and are more likely to support the autonomy of others (Deci and Ryan, 1985). Therefore, a new corporate culture needs to be developed by a firm which captures a real sense of commitment from all its employees.

Our starting point is the contention that if people are given a worthwhile goal then the need for paternalistic, autocratic management becomes an anachronism. Business, it should be recognised, is as much about human relationships as it is about outputs. The tasks organisations set cannot be specified simply in terms of actions, but require adherence to sets of values held in common between people and with the organisation. The time has gone when people will tolerate subjugation and dependence. Nor will people tolerate isolated independence. Community, in every sense of the word, calls for many different forms of solidarity and interdependence based on the common theme of sustainable development.

In the first instance we must recognise that people will only comply with the ethics and practices compatible with the aims

116

of sustainable development within the workplace, when they are persuaded that it is right and necessary so to do. This means that they must have sufficient incentives to change their behaviour and must obtain the required knowledge and skills to act according to new principles. This requires environmental education linked to social education. The former helps people to understand the natural world and to live in harmony with it. The latter imparts an understanding of the values and behaviour that are required to achieve such a state. An important point to make is that global values need to be related, within an organisational setting, to individual values in order to achieve commitment and understanding from a workforce whose starting point will always be anthropocentric.

Based on the work of the Elmwood Institute (Callenbach *et al.*, 1993) we can identify eight areas where we might start to readdress ideas, values and behaviour:

1 State of the world: the next ten years is a critical decade. The survival of humanity and of the world are at stake and the mounting global problems have reached a stage where much of the damage already done is irreversible.

2 Interconnectedness of problems: none of these global problems can be seen in isolation because they are systemic problems – interconnected and interdependent – and need a systemic approach to be understood and solved.

3 Shift from objects to relationships: the shift from the perception of the world as a machine or resource to be used, to the world as a living system is a key characteristic of a new ecological paradigm. We must move away from seeing reality as a collection of separate objects to an inseparable web of relationships.

4 Shift from parts to the whole: living systems comprise individual organisms, social systems and ecosystems, all of which are integrated. Although we can discern individual parts in any system, the nature of the whole is always different from the sum of the parts. The nature of any living thing, including a business organisation, derives from the relationships amongst its components and from the relationships of the whole system to its environment.

5 Shift from domination to partnership: the shift from domination to partnership is also central to the ecological paradigm. In the business world this translates to a shift from competition to

cooperation and from managerial hierarchy to participative arrangements.

6 Shift from structures to processes: systems thinking is process thinking and every structure is a manifestation of underlying processes. In order to understand and change systems we must understand processes.

7 Shift from individualism to integration: in a culture associated with materialism and consumption we have tended to overemphasise individualist perspectives of competition, expansion and quantity, and have neglected integration which relies on cooperation, conservation and quality.

8 Shift from growth to sustainability: the blind pursuit of unrestricted growth has been the main driving force of global environmental destruction. Within the business organisation, sustainability must replace the drive for growth and this means constantly re-examining the very ways in which the organisation conducts itself.

Strategic management begins with a vision of what the firm is and what it will become. This strategic vision which needs to encompass the principles of sustainable development will be based on a set of core values and is essentially an image that guides the firm's decision-making processes at all levels. The achievement of this sustainable vision relies on every individual participating in strategic decision-making rather than being involved in marginalist changes through improving current processes and systems. In order to induce this type of decision-making a thorough examination of an organisation's capability, personnel and existing culture needs to be undertaken. Because the nature of the business, its processes and its marketplace of the future are going to be very different, then the new investment in developing appropriate capability, organisational values, culture and appropriate individual behaviour is very important and will happen only if it is part of an overall strategic plan. This vision and its accompanying strategy to change culture is one which does not attempt to predict the future or even to identify specific environmental market opportunities way in advance. It allows a general competence to be nurtured based around individual commitment, production and service flexibility and an ultimate goal of creating a sustainable organisation. This provides an organisation with a clear identity along with the satisfaction of being able to realign products, processes or systems.

## THE CULTURE CHANGE PROGRAMME

Post and Altman (1991) provide some insight as to how formidable the cultural barriers are for implementing sustainable strategies in organisations. In their research of a range of firms, they conclude that long-term adoption of sustainability strategies will require a 'third-order change' in the culture of organisations. First-order change (developing new ways to reinforce current objectives, values, norms, structures, etc.) and second-order change (purposely modifying current objectives, values, norms, structures, etc.) are the normal focuses of a traditional organisation's change efforts. A TQM approach to change would clearly fall within the second-order change bracket. However, third-order change is a different story. It requires the organisation to adopt a completely new culture. First-order and second-order changes are linear in nature, requiring that organisations do basically the same things they are currently doing, only better. However, third-order change is discontinuous change that requires the organisation to achieve an entirely different qualitative state (Bartunek and Moch, 1987).

In order to invoke a creative tension to change, everybody within the organisation must be dissatisfied with the current strategy. But to introduce a new order of things is difficult and requires a considerable amount of bravery on the part of owners and managers. In the words of Machiavelli:

> And one should bear in mind that there is nothing more difficult to execute, nor more dubious of success, nor more dangerous to administer than to introduce a new order of things; for he who introduces it has all those who profit from the old order as his enemies, and he has only lukewarm allies in all those who might profit from the new. This lukewarmness partly stems from fear of their adversaries who have the law on their side, and partly from scepticism of men, who do not truly believe in new things unless they have actually had personal experience of them.
>
> (*The Prince*, 1513)

It seems logical to think that the power and status gained by top management through implementing current environmental strategies have such an extrinsically motivating addictive effect that people do not want to give these up readily. Managers who understand the concept of sustainable development know that the concept is synonymous with participation and cooperation. But, in turn, these often alien concepts remove a degree of power from managers and can question their very existence and it is no surprise that this should lead to inertia. Managers therefore need to be convinced in the first place that a radical change in corporate culture and in the ultimate goals of the organisation are in their best interests. The question remains as to who precisely is going to undertake such an evangelical task.

To an extent, therefore, managers have to rethink their own perception of reality and their role in a new corporate order. Ornstein and Ehrlich (1990) contend that people need to take advantage of the flexibility and trainability of the human mind in order to achieve the necessary changes to their mental pictures of reality. Arguably, humans are the most adaptable of the species and they have the potential to synthesise large amounts of information. Education about the problems faced by humankind is important, but education about the way people think may be even more important. If people could learn how they learn, if they could understand how their perceptions influence their view of the world and their reactions to it, and how the very language they use is restrictive, then they would be better equipped to modify their cognitive structures to fit the demands of their current environment. Changing cognitive structures, of course, means changing values. Adequately including sustainable development into the mental pictures that people use in making strategic decisions can be achieved only by refocusing their perceptions on gradual, long-term processes.

Asking a basic question such as 'what do you stand for?' simultaneously with 'what business are you in?' provides an indication to the individual/organisational/global purpose, and as such, it forms a direct link between ethical reasoning and strategic reasoning (Freeman and Gilbert, 1988). Philosophically, when an individual or a firm asks itself what it stands for and then consciously searches for the answer, it has an opportunity to gain a clear, in-depth understanding of the extent to which principles of and values associated with sustainable development form the foundation of his/her/its own ethical system. Our argument here is that significant clarification and modification of values will be necessary for most firms (including TQM organisations) that wish to develop and implement true sustainability strategies and intents.

Strong cultures are identified when the values expressed by individuals throughout the firm are well defined and are the same throughout the organisation or congruent both horizontally and vertically (Deal and Kennedy, 1982). Most people are aware of the many environmental and equality issues but few organisations have given their staff the opportunity to share their perceptions, to test the accuracy of their opinions and to relate their concerns to their business. This will provide a clearer understanding of the effectiveness of company policies and practices towards sustainable development. Without this kind of initiative, staff are likely to arrive at their own conclusions which will influence what they say to their work colleagues and to their family and friends. At best any negative views they may have will affect morale adversely, and at worst could, through time, damage the corporate image and the ability to recruit and retain good people. Therefore, the clarity, relevance and holistic focus of culture are crucial to the likelihood of producing a commitment to change.

Figure 6.1 provides the basis for examining the culture change process. In order to achieve a commitment towards this vision, a change programme must consider values at three different levels. Starting initially with the global and ending with the individual, it is important to note that as each layer's values are considered, the depth of understanding that is required increases. Moreover, this is a building process, where the ease of understanding becomes easier and more relevant to the individual as he or she moves from level to level. As soon as all three levels are understood, the process of decision making needs to be examined. This process links values to behaviour. A re-examination of values and the very ways in which decisions are made are therefore at the heart of the culture change programme. This provides the vehicle for all other ecological and sustainable strategies which can be seen as encapsulating the move towards the sustainable organisation.

## GLOBAL VALUES

Although sustainable development seems to be universally thought of as a 'good thing', nobody seems to agree on a universal definition for sustainable development, never mind its associated values. The term has been criticised as ambiguous and open to a

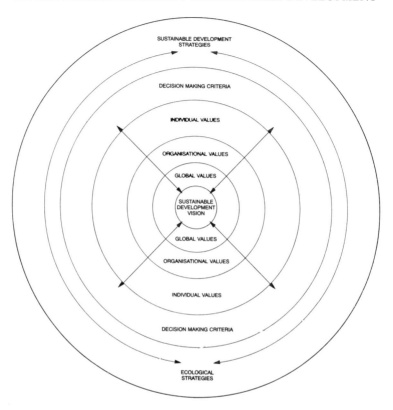

*Figure 6.1* The culture change process

wide range of interpretations, many of which are contradictory. The confusion has been caused because 'sustainable development', 'sustainable growth' and 'sustainable use' have been used interchangeably, as if their meanings were the same. They are not. 'Sustainable growth' is a contradiction in terms: nothing physical can grow indefinitely. 'Sustainable use' is applicable only to renewable resources: it means using them at rates within their capacity for renewal (IUCN, UNEP, WWF, 1991). This ambiguity is perhaps one reason why industry has applied only one ingredient to the recipe of sustainable development, which is environmental protection. This term itself is ambiguous, however (Roome, 1992), thus compounding the problem to one that seems to industry to be too complex to devise a whole cultural change programme around.

However, global values must consider a wider definition of sustainable development and this must incorporate the environment, equity and futurity. These have been discussed earlier in the book and that will not be repeated here. Nevertheless an excellent model for reconsidering our global values is provided by Agenda 21.

Agenda 21, the global plan of action adopted at the Earth Summit in Rio de Janeiro, recognises that given the nature of the problems which now confront us as a community of nations and peoples, we are now more than ever bound together by a common destiny. Solutions to these problems will have to be found at an international level. The solutions to the global problems require action at a local level, including the level of the firm. We therefore need to consider our values and attitudes towards global problems and make a transition to sustainable forms of development and lifestyle.

Agenda 21 explains that population, consumption and technology are the primary driving forces in environmental change. It shows that there are significant roles to be played by everyone: governments, business people, trade unions, scientists, teachers, indigenous people, women, youth and children. Agenda 21 does not shun business although it makes us think about the ways in which we do business. A full consideration of the message of Agenda 21 must therefore be at the heart of a reconsideration of global values.

A major theme of Agenda 21 is the need to eradicate poverty by giving poor people more access to the resources they need to live sustainably. By adopting Agenda 21, industrialised countries recognised that they have a greater role in cleaning up the environment than poor nations, who produce relatively less pollution. Whilst Agenda 21 recognises that sustainable development is primarily the responsibility of governments, these efforts require the broadest possible public participation and the active involvement of businesses.

Agenda 21 lays out a seven-point plan for business and industry and this provides only the starting point for changing values and perceptions within the organisation. It argues that business and industry should:

- develop policies that result in operations and products that have lower environmental impacts;

- ensure responsible and ethical management of products and processes from the point of view of health, safety and the environment;
- make environmentally sound technologies available to affiliates in developing countries without prohibitive charges;
- encourage overseas affiliates to modify procedures in order to reflect local ecological conditions and share information with governments;
- create partnerships to help people in smaller companies learn business skills;
- establish national councils for sustainable development, both in the formal business community and in the informal sector, which includes small-scale businesses, such as artisans;
- increase research and development of environmentally sound technologies and environmental management systems.

Agenda 21 also recognises that it is workers who will be most affected by the changes needed in industry to bring about a sustainable future. Trade unions, which have experience in dealing with industrial change, will therefore have a vital role to play. Governments, business and industry must foster the active and informed participation of workers and trade unions in shaping and implementing environment and development strategies. These strategies will affect employment policies, industrial strategies, labour adjustment programmes and technology transfers.

Unions and employers need to design joint environmental policies, and set priorities to improve the working environment and the overall environmental performance of businesses. Trade unions should develop their own sustainable development policies and take a wider perspective than the simple protection of their own members. For labour to fully support sustainable development, governments and employers should promote workers' rights to freedom of association and the right to organise.

## ORGANISATIONAL VALUES

The basic assumptions people make about the world determine the things they value, the things they pay attention to, and, ultimately, the things they do. In other words, human consciousness rests on the basic assumptions that people make about the world around them. The basic assumptions people make about business form the foundation for an organisation's culture (Schein, 1985). Thus developing consciousness towards sustainability in business organisations means changing many of the basic assumptions on which businesses are founded (Stead and Stead, 1992). An understanding of the global values outlined above gives rise to three closely related organisational values:

## 1 Profits out, ethics in

Sustainability has to be seen as within the intrinsic business concepts like profit and loss, debt and equity, capital and cost, that make our system work. What many believe to be the most significant transition from the old to the new sustainable management paradigm is the shifting perspective from the profit motive. However, many executives are motivated by short term profits through some combination of selfishness, greed and power-seeking. Whether driven by such motives or trapped in old-fashioned capitalist ideology, such people seem unable to realise what are actually their own long-term interests, as well as those of their fellow humans and of the planet. They need to become aware that it may be necessary to sacrifice considerable short-term gains in order to secure long-term benefits. One difficulty that more progressive business managers face today in trying to shift to a longer-term approach is that it could place them at a temporary competitive disadvantage in relation to their more selfish business competitors who persist in a short-term approach. Therefore, more public encouragement is needed for public-spirited business managers (Burrows, Mayne and Newbury, 1991).

The realisation that our old values of profit and economic growth are not only unable to satisfy human needs but are also threatening our very global home, has shaken the basis of our whole society. In 1992, Martin Laing, Chairman of John Laing plc said (as one of 50 members of the Business Council For Sustainable Development):

> It has been argued that one cannot serve both the needs of industry and of the environment. I believe that this is not an impossible task. Industry can no longer afford to ignore environmental needs. Profit becomes pointless without quality of life. Financial accounts tell many stories but not all, and measuring performance by profit alone will not suffice.

However, a greener future will remain an idealistic dream unless industrialists and environmentalists meet to transform it into a reality by talking and sharing problems.

(Scmidheiny, 1992)

Serving the varied, often conflicting, needs of multiple stakeholders requires the organisation to develop multiple goals formulated in social and political as well as economic terms. Due to this need to develop multiple goals for multiple stakeholders, the management focus of organisations has become more strategic (Halal, 1986). Ansoff (1979) argues that because the strategic problems facing organisations are being complicated by increasing customer sophistication, expanding global markets, increasing environmental and social awareness, changing technology, and escalating turbulence, management processes in organisations must become more strategically focused. Halal (1986) argues that strategically managed organisations are not just companies with strategic plans. These organisations don't just have a strategy, they have a philosophy of creating strategies, adapting to the environment through innovation and entrepreneurial activity.

Ernest Bader, who founded the successful Scott Bader Ltd, took a multiple stakeholder focus almost fifty years ago, and he believed that employees were the most important of a firm's stakeholders. He argues:

The classes of persons entitled to their ... satisfactions are the owners, the customers of the products or services, and the workers. Between these three is a constant jostling ... The stake of owners and customers in a business are temporary, transient, and partial, but the employee normally gives all his working time to one business and therefore seeks in and through it a much wider personal satisfaction.

(Hoe, 1978)

Today this philosophy has been adopted by many organisations. For example, GE's new organisational philosophy focuses on the human being as the key to future productivity (Rose, 1990). Indeed, quality of work life has become a primary focus of business organisations all over the world. Freeman and Gilbert (1988) believe individual worth should be the value that forms the foundation of an organisation's principles. Their basic premise is that an individual has the basic right to pursue his or her own projects free from coercion and interference from others. Individuals are ends and never mere means to someone else's ends.

Increased stakeholder awareness and the much publicised greed of the 1980s has focused a great deal of public attention on business ethics. According to the author Thomas Wolfe we are leaving the period of money fever that was the 1980s and entering a period of moral fever (Farnham, 1991). As the 1980s came to a close, it became clear that unethical business practices were of grave concern to society. Many saw the business ethics of the 1980s as greedy, selfish distortions of the free enterprise system.

Thus ethics became another dimension of the new management paradigm that focused attention away from the profit motive. Cavanagh, Moberg and Valasquez (1981) espouse that human rights and justice must be as much a part of organisational decision making as utilitarian concerns. Freeman and Gilbert (1988) point out that all business strategies have an ethical foundation regardless of whether management is aware of it. They believe that organisations should apply ethical reasoning to their strategic decision-making processes, analysing who is affected by the decisions, how they are affected, what rights the parties have, and so on.

All of this leads to the realisation that organisations that serve the needs of the greater society in which they exist are more likely to prosper. The narrow economic niche in which business organisations once resided has expanded into a much broader societal niche (Zenisek, 1979). It is generally understood today that social performance cannot be separated from economic performance. As well as earning a profit, organisations today are expected to contribute to social welfare. Halal (1986) argues that the key to restoring economic vitality today is to recognise that social goals and profit are not only compatible, but so interdependent that the firm cannot succeed unless it unifies these two sets of concerns.

## 2 Smart growth

Another dimension that could be included in this new sustainable management paradigm is the concept of smart growth, discussed most completely by Halal (1986). He presents convincing arguments that changing economic trends (such as the decline of materialism) and increasing environmental problems are rapidly rendering hard growth (growth achieved via increases in physical commodity production) unfeasible. Smart growth involves turning today's economic and environmental problems into tomorrow's business opportunities. Economic growth in the future will occur within organisations and industries that contribute to improving the quality of life. Industries such as day care, waste management, pollution control, educational services, and information processing are likely to grow, while basic manufacturing industries will continue to decline. Thus values are changing, people in advanced economies are becoming disenchanted with growth as an end in itself, material consumption is often unsatisfying, many distrust the complexity of technology, and they fear the insidious effects of pollution. Instead, they are becoming interested in social relationships, satisfying jobs, and other aspects of the quality of life.

Halal (1986) contends that the transition from hard growth to smart growth has been a three-decade evolution that began with challenges to unlimited material progress during the student activism of the 1960s, continued during the self-examination and inner-growth period of the 1970s, and was solidified by the hard economic realities of the 1980s. This transition has led to a new, more thoughtful dream that balances the advantages of economic growth with its social costs. Halal calls this a transition from more, to better, to less. Peters (1990) agrees, suggesting that the great economies of the world cannot expect to continue to grow through greater commodity production and that the battleground has shifted from 'more, more, more' to 'better, better, better'.

## 3 Equality and democracy

We have argued earlier in the book that truly democratic values must be universally incorporated for a sustainable culture to exist. This new organisational cooperative form of politics must build on a broad consensus of basic altruistic values, social justice, and decent standards for all. This new democratic form would start by considering the true basis for democracy.

According to Burrows *et al.* (1991) a democratic order needs to have an adequate conceptual framework that would be provided by a holistic political philosophy including the following objectives:

1 unite people with a common purpose;
2 care for all people, share resources fairly, and provide everyone with a decent quality of life;

3 develop, and use constructively, the abilities of all citizens and enable them to fulfil their creative talents;

4 establish a just organisation, with a proper framework of employee rights and employee responsibilities;

5 carry out political functions at whatever scale or level is appropriate;

6 decentralise, devolve and avoid bureaucracy wherever possible.

Some important examples of inequality in the workplace are described below with emphasis on the beneficial changes that need to be made.

### Ageism

Faulkner (1980) points out that older workers are now an increasing proportion of the workforce, yet the greatest value is currently placed on the potential of younger workers. Most occupations prefer to replace their older workers, rather than use them better. Faulkner recommends that more training should be available to help older workers cope with the rundown to retirement and with retirement itself. Sometimes retraining, updating of skills, or re-employment could make the later years of work far more tolerable and worthwhile, but further research is needed to find alternative forms of employment for people approaching retirement.

Javeau (1980) rejects the idea of assessing people's fitness for work on grounds of chronological age. With ageing populations in developing countries and greatly extended life expectancy, it would be helpful to these countries and beneficial for their citizens to make better use of older people. He suggests various possibilities for pre-retirement education, retraining, and alternative work for older people including different types of socially valuable work. He condemns the current widespread view of retired people as diminished adults with reduced rights. They should be invited to participate in society, which would thereby benefit from their abilities and experience. By having opportunities to do socially valuable work, older people would be able to identify with the rest of society and find a sense of purpose and importance, instead of being relegated to the fringe of society, waiting to die in isolation (Burrows et al., 1991).

## Sexism

Women are important managers of natural resources: they can restore, sustain and create liveable and productive environments. Their skills, experience and perspectives are essential for sustainability within the workplace. As women achieve equal status, they will play a major part in reducing conflict, because they are more interested in compromise and traditionally have more empathy than men. Unfortunately, they have so far played a relatively minor role in the decision making of both the developed countries and the developing countries (Burrows *et al.*, 1991). As a consequence, many lack the opportunity for self-fulfilment, and potential contributions to the community are lost. The following initial steps (IUCN, UNEP, WWF, 1991) could help improve their status:

- recognition of the important role of women in the care and management of the environment;
- extensive consultation with women (not just educated women) to find out what their present role is, what they believe their role should be and what support they need;
- ratifying and upholding the Convention on the Elimination of All Forms of Discrimination Against Women. Legislation should ensure equal pay for equal work, equal representation of women in on-the-job training programmes, maternity leave benefits, and provisions for day care of the elderly, sick, disabled and children;
- increasing economic opportunities for women, for example, by helping women to set up their own businesses, providing training in business management, and fostering savings clubs and loan facilities for women;
- instituting reforms to give women a full voice in political, bureaucratic, and economic decision making at every level.

## Animal rights

Every life form warrants respect independently of its worth to people. Human development should not threaten the integrity of nature or the survival of other species. People should treat all creatures decently, and protect them from cruelty, avoidable suffering, and unnecessary killing. The obligation to protect all creatures from cruelty, avoidable suffering and unnecessary killing can also conflict with the requirement that no people should be deprived of its means of subsistence. The campaign against the fur trade has deprived indigenous peoples in Greenland and northern Canada of a major source (and for some communities, the only source) of income, even though they were harvesting those resources sustainably. Elephant conservation may have been more difficult in several southern African countries because they can no longer obtain a financial return from the animals they have to cull. Such conflicts reveal radically different cultural interpretations of the ethic for living sustainably. There is a vast difference between the killing of animals to sustain indigenous forms of living and testing animals to ensure that make-up which we use will not give us a rash. The answers to conflicts over animal rights lie not in prescriptive cause-and-effect solutions but in the very fact that the issue is being thought about, using a form of systems thinking and decision making which has sustainable development as its vision (IUCN, UNEP, WWF, 1991).

## INDIVIDUAL VALUES

Any acceptable vision of sustainable development must include fair treatment of today's population through an appreciation of their individual aspirations to achieve a better quality of life, defined widely. Sustainable development as yet has not been articulated in terms of what each employee in an organisation can aspire to (self-determination, individuality, quality of life), how they are going to achieve these individual aspirations (unleashing creativity) and the mechanisms to achieve such a situation (participation, cooperation, empowerment, etc).

Understanding of global and organisational values gives rise to the following five closely related individual values.

### 1 Smallness

Schumacher (1979) promoted the concept of 'small is beautiful' and he suggested that modern industrial society was living under three dangerous illusions:

1 Unlimited growth is possible in a finite world;
2 There are unlimited numbers of people willing to perform mindless work for moderate salaries;
3 Science can be used to solve all social problems.

To him, these illusions were paths to resource depletion, environmental degradation, worker alienation, and violence. Large organisations inhibit freedom, creativity, and human dignity. The only way to reverse this in vast organisations is to achieve smallness within the large bureaucracy (Schumacher, 1973). This is precisely what organisations are accepting as they become ever more flexible (Welford and Prescott, 1994). Peters and Waterman (1982) argue that small in almost every case is beautiful and that small, quality, excitement, autonomy and efficiency, are all words that belong on the same side of the coin.

Economic scale is ultimately defined by the amount of energy and resources that are transformed from their natural state into outputs, including wastes (Daly and Cobb, 1989). Thus valuing smallness has implications for every aspect of the economic cycle. At the production end of the cycle, smallness helps managers account more accurately for the value of the scarce resources that form the foundation of all economic capital. Smallness encourages strategic decision makers to implement policies aimed at using as little as possible of the Earth's non-renewable resources. Expanding on the concept of smallness for organisational decision making, Morgan (1986) proposes that coordination should be based on the development of shared values and shared understanding, with managers developing skills of 'remote management,' such as 'helicoptering' and 'managing through the umbilical cord'. In other words managers must become skilled in designing and managing systems of small decentralised parts that are self-organising and have a large degree of independence and self-determination. Management must become much more concerned with empowerment than with close supervision and control. Organisations applying smallness with a systemic perspective of the whole to their strategic decisions are more likely to focus attention on searching for ways to save energy and to use more renewable energy sources in the production and distribution of their products and services. Smallness will also encourage organisations to look for ways to reduce the materials that go into their products, including packaging.

Valuing smallness in the production of goods and services has tremendous implications for the technologies used by organisations. Renewable energy technologies would obviously emanate from such a value. Peters and Waterman (1982) repeatedly found that the efficiency provided by smallness was consistently profitable for the companies they investigated. Organisations are discovering the economic benefits of small work teams, energy efficiency, and smart growth; industries (such as waste management) that deal with the deleterious effects of bigness show promising opportunities for the future. The premise of smallness is what Schumacher (1973) bases his five-point strategy on.

1 Large organisations should be divided into 'quasi-firms', small, autonomous teams designed to foster high levels of entrepreneurial spirit.
2 Accountability of quasi-firms to higher management should be based on a few items related to profitability. Decisions are to be made by team members in ad hoc fashion without interference from upper management; upper management steps in only if the profitability goals are not being met.
3 The quasi-firms should maintain their own economic identity; they should be allowed to have their own names and keep their own records. Their financial performance should not be merged with other units.
4 Motivation for lower-level workers can be achieved only if the job is intellectually and spiritually fulfilling with ample opportunities to participate in decisions; this can only be achieved in small, meaningful groups.
5 Top management can balance the need for employee freedom with the need for organisational control by setting broad, strategic performance targets and allowing the quasi-firms to make their own decisions within these targets.

The structure of a company organised around these principles resembles a helium balloon vendor at a carnival with a large number of balloons for sale. The vendor (who represents top management) holds the balloons from below rather than lording over them from above. Each balloon represents an autonomous unit that shifts and sways on its own within the limits defined by the vendor. Organisations should be structured, like nature, into little cells. Therefore, organisational structures should be based on a broad network design that would be stimulated by advancing communications and computer technology.

Schumacher (1979) argues that business is not there simply to produce goods, it also produces people. Organisations have the responsibility to provide quality work for employees, work that is enjoyable and that satisfies the creative and spiritual needs of employees. Schumacher goes even further:

> How do we prepare young people for the future world of
> work? . . . They should be encouraged to reject meaningless,
> boring, stultifying, or nerve-racking work in which a man (or
> woman) is made servant of a machine or a system. They
> should be taught that work is the joy of life and is needed for
> our development, but that meaningless work is an abom-
> ination.
>
> (Schumacher, 1979)

Quality work can only be found in organisations that allow human
dignity and freedom to flourish in small autonomous groups like
those described in his model. The lack of available good work in
our bureaucratised, mass-production society is the primary contributor to inflation. When there is no intrinsic fulfilment from
their job, the natural tendency is for employees to focus on getting
more compensation (money) for what they do. But to change the
nature of work will also mean changing the nature of education
which prepares people for work. Education will have to deal more
completely with traditional questions such as: What is (wo)man?
Where do we come from? What is our purpose? Only when people
find their own answers to these questions will they be able to
identify what type of work provides them with their path
to fulfilment.

A good advertisement for smallness is Richard Branson's organisation. His philosophy of motivation can be summed up under the
heading 'Small is Beautiful'. He says:

> In the early days, we could certainly not have afforded a
> lavish corporate headquarters in central London. But now we
> don't have one as a matter of choice. It's not just that people
> seem to prefer working in smaller units, but it helps to avoid
> some of the hazards of growth, and especially the tendency
> for managers to lose touch with the basics and usually the
> customers and the staff. So when one of our companies gets
> beyond a certain size, we split into smaller units. Even
> though Virgin Records was, before we sold it to Thorn EMI,
> the sixth largest record company in the world, we managed it
> through a series of semi-independent labels and subsidiaries
> in twenty countries. This 'keep it small' rule gives us the
> opportunity to pursue a policy of promoting from within
> the Group – a policy which clearly has a positive effect on
> morale. It means you can give more than the usual number of

managers the challenge and excitement of running their own business.

(Cannon, 1993)

## 2 Wholeness

Wholeness helps people remember that survival depends on successfully interacting with other living systems on the planet, because the whole cannot survive if its parts are destroyed. Further, because the whole is defined by how its parts interact with one another, valuing wholeness helps people to better perceive and attend to the relationships with other elements of the environment.

In his sixteenth-century essays, philosopher Michel de Montaigne (1958a) elegantly appealed to the need for decision makers to adopt wholeness as a value. He believed that people could comprehend the true impact of their decisions only if they accounted for the wholeness of the Earth and their role in it. On this point, he said:

> Whoever calls to his mind, as in a picture, the great image of our mother nature in all her majesty; whoever reads in her face her universal and constant variety; whoever sees himself in it... like a dot made by a very fine pencil; he alone estimates things according to their true proportions.
>
> (Montaigne, 1958a)

Montaigne also believed that decision makers needed to realise that when they made decisions, their actions would always have an influence (usually negative) on someone else and/or something else:

> No profit can be made except at another's expense... As I was reflecting on this, the fancy came upon me that here nature is merely following her habitual policy. For natural scientists hold that the birth, nourishment, and growth of each thing means the change and decay of something else.
>
> (Montaigne, 1958b)

Thus Montaigne captured two reasons as to why valuing wholeness is advantageous for strategic decision makers wishing to achieve a sustainable balance between economic success and environmental protection. Firstly, a value of wholeness is of tremendous benefit to novel, creative efforts. New products, new services, and new methods can all spring from the value of wholeness. Thus valuing

135

wholeness can contribute significantly to a firm's economic success in a very competitive world. Secondly, wholeness develops an understanding of where the organisation fits into ecosystems, and that most organisational actions have some negative effect on other systems of the planet. Wholeness can give managers an ecological perspective on which to base their decisions. They will be more likely to examine the impact of their decision on other people, communities, societies, and the Earth. No doubt, wholeness is a value that, if adopted by decision makers in organisations, would contribute significantly to sustaining the Earth's ecological balance.

## 3 Posterity

'We didn't inherit the Earth from our parents; we borrowed it from our children.' This well-known Kenyan proverb clearly describes why posterity is an important value in order to achieve sustainability. Valuing posterity, believing that future generations of human beings are prominent factors in strategic decisions, can be instrumental in attaining a sustainable economic and ecological balance. According to Speth (1990), sustainability can be achieved only if society can attain economic development that meets the needs of present generations without compromising the ability of future generations to meet their own needs.

The future does not look as bright for the younger generation of children as it did for the previous one, and the environment is a major reason why. An image of society based on unlimited economic growth has caused humankind to fall into ecological traps, raising serious concerns about the quality of life for our future generations. Assuming social scientists are correct in concluding that a positive image for future generations is critical to the health of a society, then there is every reason to be concerned. Ornstein and Ehrlich (1990) make it clear that people's picture of the future will have to change drastically if they wish to develop a positive view for their children and their children's children. It may help if people realised how old (or young) humankind really is. The Earth is 4.5 billion years old, but human civilisations did not appear until ten thousand years ago, written histories began only around five thousand years ago, and the industrial age has barely reached three hundred years. Milbrath (1989) effectively demonstrates the significance of these time periods by envisioning a one-year film encompassing the Earth's entire history. If the film began on 1 January, dinosaurs would not appear until 13 December, mammals would enter the scene on 15 December, and Homo sapiens would make their film debut at 11 minutes before midnight of 31 December. Civilised human activity would not emerge until the last two minutes of the film, recorded history would begin one minute before the curtain comes down, the industrial age would dominate only the last one and a half seconds, and our own lifetimes would flicker by during the final half second of the film. Maybe this film can put what is called long-range planning into its proper perspective.

Valuing posterity is an important ingredient in effectively managing the change and turbulence that all organisations now face and will continue to face in the twenty-first century. Adopting posterity as a value encourages business organisations to develop a vision of what they are and what they want to be. Having a clear vision of the future has proven to be a critical factor in successful organisations. Visions serve as common denominators around which strategic decisions are shaped and implemented. Shared visions in organisations encourage employees to think strategically; when strategic thinking is a part of organisational culture, the company is better prepared to manage its opportunities and threats in ways that are advantageous to its survival and prosperity (Ernst and Baginski, 1989/1990).

In addition to supporting economic sustainability, posterity is also important in order to achieve ecosystem sustainability. In strategic decision making, taking future generations into account significantly influences a wide range of choices. If managers believe that clean water, clean air, abundant resources, and natural beauty are the birthright of all generations, not just their own, then the decisions they make are bound to better reflect a concern for the Earth. The Iroquois Indians of North America had a seven-generation planning horizon; they tried to predict the effects of their decisions for the next seven generations to follow. This type of long-range planning by business organisations would tremendously enhance the sustainability of our small planet.

## 4 Community

Communities are not simply groups of people occupying patches of land. They are complex social systems composed of diverse individuals and organisations. Communities share at least three characteristics:

1 the members are conscious of their relationships with others in the community;
2 the members are conscious of the limits of the community; and
3 the members are conscious of the differences between themselves and those who live outside the community (Daly and Cobb, 1989).

Thus, although communities usually share a common geography, the essence of a community lies primarily in the complex cognitive networks that form around the values and expectations of the individuals and organisations that comprise it. As Etzioni (1991) says, communities are identified by their 'sense of we-ness'.

Because communities are more cognitive than physical, they exist in many forms. Terms like local community, business community, religious community, and European Community all fit into the definition of community. In this sense, there is no need to differentiate between the terms community and society; communities simply represent the underlying social form on which societies are based (Daly and Cobb, 1989). Etzioni (1991) argues that communities exist like Chinese nesting boxes, in that smaller ones (e.g. families) are embedded in more encompassing ones (e.g. villages) and these in still more encompassing ones (e.g. counties) and so it goes on.

The shared values and expectations that make up the essence of communities lead to their strongest influence, establishing ethical standards. Heisenberg (1985) contends that ethics is the basis for the communal life of people. Communities themselves have no power to coerce people to behave in socially acceptable ways (communities may have police forces with coercive powers, but the powers of the police result from shared community values for law and order, public safety, etc.); however, the moral codes of communities serve as public barometers by which the behaviours of individual members are judged and controlled (Etzioni, 1991).

Many ecological problems stem from the belief that serving one's self-interests necessarily results in the collective good (the neo-classical doctrine of radical individualism). The opposite notion is subscribed to here. Individuals, organisations, and economies are parts of a greater community; thinking only of themselves leads to individual actions that are detrimental to the encompassing systems of which they are a part. Daly and Cobb (1989) argue that in the real world the self-contained individual does not exist. They reject the idea that organisations are like Robinson Crusoe, earning their way solely on their own guile, in favour of the belief that organisations are integral parts of interlocking communal systems composed of individuals, families, towns, cities, nations, international coalitions, and ecological systems bound by a common desire for quality of life.

Thus managers who value the greater community are better equipped to make decisions compatible with achieving sustainability. Those who adopt a value for community will better understand that the survival of their organisation depends on their ability to serve the needs and follow the ethical standards of the more comprehensive communities to which they belong. Managers who value community will also be aware that the community's survival depends on business organisations that contribute to a viable economy. Thus, they are more conscious of the interconnections between their decisions and the quality of life in the communities in which they operate. They recognise that their organisations can prosper over the long run only if the community can maintain a balance between a healthy natural environment, ample opportunities for human development and fulfilment, a meaningful code of ethics, and a healthy system of economic activity. Accordingly, managers who value community are likely to benefit from numerous economic advantages such as customer loyalty, positive public image and employee commitment as well as contributing to the protection of the natural environment.

## 5 Quality

As a value supporting sustainability, quality is essentially the corollary of smallness. That is, changing from valuing bigness to valuing smallness dictates a value change from quantity to quality. Once organisations adopt the philosophy that how well products are made and how well customers are served is more important than how many products are produced and how many are sold to customers, then the proper scale of their operations can be defined by something other than physical growth: It can be defined by an overriding image of quality based on the perceptions of customers. As organisations learn that they cannot be all things to all people, smallness will very likely result from a focus on quality. When quality is the nucleus around which organisations revolve, they are likely to adopt a scale of operations small enough to focus on developing individual relationships within their stakeholder network. Further, as the United Kingdom has learned (often painfully) from the Japanese, improved customer loyalty, more stable supplier relationships, more participative interactions among organisational members, and improved operational efficiency are all possible outcomes for organisations that adopt quality as a key value in their strategic decision-making processes.

The value of quality best supports sustainability if it includes three basic dimensions:

1 Quality of products and services: quality products and services also support ecological sustainability because they last longer, are worth repairing, and can be exchanged more readily in second-hand markets. Furthermore, high conformance quality (quality based on carefully and precisely conforming to internal specifications) reduces costs because of lower scrap, less rework and less time responding to complaints. Therefore ecological benefits stem from a reduction in wastes and end user disposal. A preponderance of durable, long-lasting products in the economic system will help to reduce the perception that constant style changes are necessary.

2 Quality work: quality products and services are simply not possible without quality work. As discussed above, structuring jobs around the concept of quality work, work that satisfies human needs as well as organisational needs, can improve the quality of products and services. This is because quality work encourages employees to be creative and to contribute their best efforts to accomplishing the organisation's economic goals and objectives. Further, the psychological satisfaction that people derive from quality work often reduces their desire to consume more and more goods. Satisfaction derived from work is of equal importance with satisfaction derived from consumption.

3 Quality of life: achieving sustainability via quality is also enhanced by valuing the quality of life in general; valuing the quality of life encourages managers to recognise that all of their stakeholders have rights to physical well-being, long-lasting happiness, personal fulfilment, and a hopeful future (Milbrath, 1989). Such a value focuses the attention of managers on how intricately interwoven economic sustainability and ecosystem

140

sustainability really are. Valuing quality of life brings a wide variety of economic and environmental issues to the attention of organisations, including job design, organisational reward systems, employee health and safety, shareholder wealth, community economic development, pollution, waste control, and so on.

Putting all the components of global, organisational and individual values together allows us to redraw our culture change process diagram. Figure 6.2 therefore maps out the actions required to change to values consistent with sustainable development. Having considered the need to readdress values within the organisation we need to move on to consider the important issue of decision making.

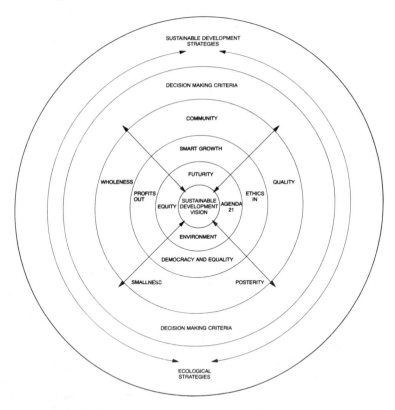

*Figure 6.2* Principal elements in the culture change process

## DECISION-MAKING CRITERIA

In chapter 4 it was suggested that a move towards ecological management practices and strategies consistent with sustainable development required systemic thinking. Intuitive and creative thinking are paramount here and coordination is achieved implicitly through informal shared understandings. Norms are implicit in what people do rather than explicit in written job descriptions. There ought to be little formal structure. Indeed systems thinking requires a shift away from structures towards processes. The absence of formality which needs to be developed within a participatory organisation enables personal ties and mutual commitment to be developed.

Decision making founded in systemic thinking represents a shift in the way that managers think about the problems they face. According to Senge (1990) the old management paradigm was dominated by linear thought processes that dictated that managers view organisational problems as cause-and-effect chains. He argues that linear thinking in organisations leads to seven organisational learning disabilities. These are:

1  thinking in terms of individual jobs rather than in terms of the whole organisation;
2  blaming problems on people or things that are outside the organisation;
3  believing that organisations can always solve their problems by taking aggressive action against whatever external force they believe is causing problems;
4  becoming fixated on specific, sudden events;
5  being unable to perceive threats that result from slow, gradual processes;
6  believing that they immediately experience the consequences of their decisions; and,
7  operating under the myth that management teams interact cross-functionally to solve problems when, in reality, these teams often spend tremendous energy defending the self-interests of individual members.

Such outcomes are piecemeal, waste resources and lead to sub-optimal decisions being made. Yet they exist in many organisations and we all have experienced them at some time. Linear thinking must therefore be replaced with holistic, systemic thinking in order to allow organisations to see the broad, dynamic, recurring processes that underlie organisational problems. Systemic thinking allows organisations to understand that circular rather than linear relationships are at the heart of most organisational problems. Senge (1990) contends that reality is made up of circles. In systems thinking it is an axiom that every influence is both cause and effect. Once organisations begin to think about mutual causality rather than straightforward cause and effect lines, then identifying the true value of relationships amongst the key variables and agents involved in a situation becomes possible. Senge (1990) provides a simple example of how this circular pattern works in business: a company produces a superior product that leads to satisfied customers; the satisfied customers pass the word about the high quality of the product to others; demand for the product then rises; the company produces more products, which leads to more satisfied customers, which leads to more word-of-mouth about the high quality of the product, and so on. In this way, the firm grows rapidly. However, if the firm does not recognise the circular relationships among the variables, then demand could begin to exceed the firm's ability to produce the demanded number of products and still continue to meet its high-quality standards. If this occurs, then the firm may cut corners on quality in order to meet demand, and the cycle will reverse itself. Customers will buy the lower quality products, become dissatisfied, and spread the word that quality of the product is below par. All of a sudden, sales will begin to fall. The key to avoiding this problem is recognising the circular, holistic relationships amongst quality, customer satisfaction, positive image, and sales.

In a similar way, systemic thinking helps people recognise that all the Earth's living systems are parts of a supranational ecological system. It drives people to better perceive and attend to the relationships with other elements of the environment.

Therefore, systems thinking provides managers with the broad perspective they need to remain competitive in today's living, global network of complex, dynamic business activity. Thinking of the world as an interconnected whole provides a much clearer understanding of the cooperative, participative relationships that organisations need to develop with their employees, customers, suppliers, and other stakeholders. Systemic approaches to environmental improvement are fundamental, therefore. As an approach to decision making we need to put a renewed emphasis on creativity,

143

action, consumer awareness, ownership, and a talent to perceive common interests and turn them into alliances. Let us deal with each of these in turn.

## Creativity

Creativity is important in all areas of management but the particular challenges inherent in moving towards sustainability require creativity to be encouraged and supported at both the individual and group levels. This approach means that we must recognise that it is systems that control events. When we fail to grasp the systemic source of problems, we are left to treat symptoms rather than eliminate underlying causes. It is important to avoid focusing on snapshots of isolated parts of the system, wondering why our deepest problems never seem to get solved. Raising the ecological performance of a business and its products needs constructive invention, not the common piecemeal approach of eliminating suspect ingredients or consuming less. The real environmental quality improvement delivers more performance from less energy and raw materials.

Individual creativity can be developed. Many techniques of creative thought have been devised, and some of them have been outlined by Koestler (1964), Mayne (1965), Rickards (1974) and Ochse (1990). Various techniques for developing group creativity are to be found by reading Jungk and Mullert (1987) and Drambo (1988).

## Action

It is often argued that business must have a proactive stance on the environment. This means approaching challenges actively rather than passively. But still, so many companies drive towards the future whilst looking through the rearview mirror. This must be overcome by adopting an attitude of anticipating and confronting future challenges rather than managing in relation to events that have already occurred.

## Awareness of the needs of consumers

Close awareness of the needs of customers and consumers is required and this must be an integral part of market research (see chapter 7). Support from outside organisations, most notably local conservation groups and national pressure groups, increases the credibility of the organisation, as this shows an understanding of the intensity of consumers' concern about the environment. An 'outside-in' management philosophy is needed where managers relate to the environment in terms of what is necessary to meet the challenge of new technologies, and the evolving demands of external stakeholders, especially customers and potential customers.

## Ownership

All employees must be encouraged to feel ownership of the company's environmental behaviour and environmental strategy. Changing a company's environmental behaviour cannot just be a separate, staff function. Senior management has to set environmental quality high on every middle manager's priority list. Then these individual managers will find the opportunities, and go after the necessary action steps with the same vigour that they pursue product improvements, marketing, volume, and profit opportunities.

## Making alliances through community action

Environmental improvement often needs the combined effort of several companies, a whole industry and government. In particular, sustainability cannot be achieved if appropriate environmental strategies exist in only a few companies, industries, or nations. Managers need to use the community instrumental value, understanding that individuals, organisations, and economies are parts of a greater community (thinking only of themselves leads to individual actions that are detrimental to the encompassing systems of which they are a part). Daly and Cobb (1989) argue that in the real world the self-contained individual does not exist. They reject the idea that organisations are earning their way solely on their own guile, in favour of the belief that organisations are integral parts of interlocking communal systems composed of individuals, families, towns, cities, nations, international coalitions, and ecological systems bound by a common desire for a high quality of life. It is not enough for a company to change its own products and processes. Success depends on a management's ability to mobilise other organisations to change their thinking and their actions.

Technology cooperation between firms, with benefits for all

parties, is an effective way to enhance both productivity and environmental quality. Working with suppliers to ensure quality control and improved environmental performance can help purchasing firms as well as the suppliers. Industry trade associations can also act as catalysts to help an entire industrial sector.

## MOTIVATING CHANGE

Throughout this book it has been stressed that a move towards more sustainable ways of doing business requires the participation of everyone associated with a company. If there are members of management or the workforce who are not convinced of the need for ecological management strategies then they must be motivated to change. Unless there is a personal commitment to change, then the culture change programme can only fail.

Formulating and implementing change will ultimately be the responsibility of management, but they will find their task easier if they adopt systemic thinking and a cooperative and participatory style with employees. The focus should be on empowering individuals and harnessing their individual energies for change. This means recognising people's full potentials, respecting their ability to make sound decisions, trusting their skills and experience, emphasising intuition and increasing flexibility. Human relations need to be emphasised and managers should develop their powers of empathy.

When it comes to decision making, not only should as wide a constituency as possible be involved, but they must also be provided with sufficient good quality information for those decisions to be quality decisions. People like to feel valued and needed and this will always be the case in a sustainable organisation. Such respect for the individual is a critical motivator in its own right. When a decision generates positive results, for example, this should be widely reported and the due recognition given to all those people who were part of that decision-making process.

The strongest motivating force for a company will be in the personal integrity of its managers and employees. As ecological awareness and personal integrity become stronger, workers will no longer wish to be associated with ecologically destructive processes and products. The firm will therefore be forced to re-orientate its business. This push will have come from within though, and it will be more powerful because of that. In time, therefore, high ecological standards will shape the direction of the company and go hand-in-hand with high quality work. A shift from quantity to quality will take place.

The new ecological paradigm is a holistic one, viewing the world and nature as interdependent and interconnected systems. Such a holistic view means that the firm should also address the whole-person concept as part of its training and motivation. Holistic management requires people to look closely at themselves, to spend time on their own personal development and to look closely at their relationships with the other people around them. The Elmwood Institute (Callenbach et al., 1993) suggests that training and motivation programmes involve people in addressing feeling through an experiential approach to ecology, through training in systems thinking; addressing the sense of responsibility for one's health, one's fellow human beings, other living creatures and future generations; addressing judgement by developing the ability to assess and select ecological options; and, addressing action through constant encouragement to put new insights and decisions into practice.

## CONCLUSIONS

The thrust of any culture change consistent with the aim of creating a sustainable organisation lies in a shift of business style from a management-controlled, short-term, planning philosophy to one which bases its strategy on a long-term, democratic, creative, systemic form of decision making based on the recognition of values at the global, organisational and individual levels. The scale and nature of this third-order culture change is such that the strategic approach can be adopted successfully only if staff at all levels are involved. It may take some time to build the understanding and commitment of all employees but without it, the achievement of the desired goals remains an illusion. In order to gain a true commitment to sustainable development strategies, a culture has to be defined, through an examination of the instrumental values required to be owned by each employee. It has been postulated that sustainable development global values need to move beyond the usual environmental concerns, into the realms of equity, environmental protection and futurity. They then need to be expressed in both organisational and individual senses for people to understand the collective gain but also their own individual gain (quality of life, individuality and self-determination).

Culture change is not a once-and-for-all process, however. Most people require time to think through the implications of a more sustainable future. They need to come to terms with what is involved for them personally and to relate this to how they work with others. This cannot be done in a didactic way, when it is unlikely to have any real effect. Culture change comes about through involvement and experiencing what it is like to live and work in accordance with the culture that is desired for the future health of any business.

Sustainable development at the level of businesses is going to be achieved, not through piecemeal approaches, but through a much more radical form of organisation that uses its people to their full potential. This can only be achieved through a new culture based on clearly defined values which produce self-determined creative behaviour. Managing to bind people together around a common identity and sense of destiny is one of the major factors for success. All too often, a company's shared vision has revolved around the charisma of a leader, or around a crisis that galvanises everyone together. Sustainability must become an individual's vision as well as being a shared vision.

# 7

# GREEN MARKETING AND ECO-LABELLING

## INTRODUCTION

The concept of marketing is not new, emerging in the early part of the 1900s in response to changes in the economic and competitive environment. New mass production techniques increased the supply of goods to the point where they overtook demand and therefore producers had to find ways of selling their goods and keep their mass production systems at full capacity (Peattie, 1992). Mass production processes tended initially to standardise products but businesses soon began to see the need to differentiate themselves from their competitors and to match their product ranges to their customers' needs.

Many definitions of marketing exist. They include those which are expressly concerned with ensuring that consumers get what they want:

> Marketing is a social process by which individuals and groups obtain what they need and want through creating and exchanging products and values with others.
>
> (Kotler, 1984: 4)

and extend to those which are all-embracing:

> Marketing is so basic that it cannot be considered a separate function.... It is the whole business seen from the customer's point of view.
>
> (Drucker, 1973: 6)

Because we wish to take a holistic view to business in this book, marketing must be seen as akin to 'total management', embracing a wide array of disciplines from the inception and creation of new products, cost management and the pricing of goods, through logistics management and on to promotion, sales and after-service which is the front line between the firm and its customers.

Marketing is dependent on the structures, processes and systems within which the firm operates. This includes the competitive, economic, political, social and cultural spheres to which the marketing strategy has to be matched. To many therefore, green marketing is a simple and natural extension of the marketing process, recognising the importance of environmental and ecological considerations at every level of the organisation and in the marketplace. It is argued here, however, that rather than an extension to traditional marketing, green marketing represents a discontinuous shift in corporate philosophy. Green marketing is ethical, ecological and compatible with sustainable development. It represents a culture change which emphasises cooperation rather than competition, eliminates sales hype and provides honest information to the consumer. Its tools of analysis are compatible with life cycle assessment (discussed in chapter 5) and its selling techniques are non-stereotypical, non-exploitative and open to public scrutiny. Whilst many academics espousing the theory of marketing might claim that that is precisely what any marketing strategy ought to be about, the rhetoric hardly accords with the reality.

The context in which the business operates has been changed because of a growing public familiarity with environmental issues. This is likely to continue and the consumer is going to be more and more sophisticated in his or her choices and in what he or she believes from the corporate message. It is likely that people will become less trusting of companies, and indeed catastrophes such as the Exxon Valdez oil spill, the Chernobyl incident and Bhopal only highlight to consumers that much of the world's ecological destruction has been caused directly by the drive towards more and more output without regard to ecological protection and safety.

This situation means that the way the firm communicates with the outside world through its products, services and other activities is going to have to be more open and honest. Moreover, firms will have to recognise that consumers will switch away from their products if they believe that the company is not acting in a reasonable way. Callenbach et al. (1993) report that 25 per cent of American consumers claim that they have changed their buying choices because of negative impressions of particular companies. Many companies are thinking much harder about the ways they are portraying themselves and building ethical and ecological considerations into the communications strategies.

The green marketing function is therefore a very wide one. It must encompass all the operations and activities of the firm, emphasise the life cycle impact of a product and look carefully at an organisation's corporate image. It must be involved in setting ecological criteria for product design, it must carefully consider packaging and promotion of products and it should be open and honest about the achievements of the firm from an ecological perspective and be able to demonstrate commitment to do even more.

The marketing and communications function is also accentuated by the increasing use of standardised and certificated eco-labels. The European Union's eco-label was always supposed to replace the labels which companies awarded to themselves, often on spurious environmental grounds. New labels ought to be capable of guiding consumers towards the purchase of less damaging products, although the criteria on which they are based need to be carefully examined in the context of sustainable development.

Advertising policies will also have to adapt to changing conditions, a more ethical approach to business and an increased distaste of stereotypical or offensive images. Advertising will have to be more specific and all claims will have to be capable of proof to overcome the chronic public scepticism resulting from traditional approaches to marketing and dishonest environmental claims.

## TRADITIONAL APPROACHES TO GREEN MARKETING

Authors such as Peattie (1992) see green marketing as a new variation of traditional marketing techniques and strategies. He defines green marketing as 'the management process responsible for identifying, anticipating and satisfying the requirements of customers and society, in a profitable and sustainable way' (p. 11) and which is seen as different from more conventional approaches in four main ways:

- it has an open-ended rather than a long-term perspective;
- it focuses more strongly on the natural environment;

- it treats the environment as something which has an intrinsic value over and above its usefulness to society; and
- it focuses on global concerns rather than those of particular societies.

Such an approach mirrors the marginalist type of approaches which we identified in the first chapter of this book. Moreover, it is an approach which invites companies to pay lip-service to environmentalism because it never spells out precise ecological criteria. Simply focusing on the natural environment and on global concerns (both wide undefined concepts) will be interpreted by many businesses in a narrow way and will hardly be reflected in a 'business as usual' scenario.

More enlightened commentators such as Coddington (1993) see green marketing as requiring two main features:

- an environmental perspective which appreciates the effect of corporate actions on the environment; and
- environmental commitment where the organisation resolves to become an environmental steward and to reflect that posture in all its actions.

The elements of this approach are laid out in Figure 7.1.

Having the right perspective requires an understanding of the severity and the breadth of the environmental crisis both in relation to physical issues such as air, water and land degradation and wider but related issues such as animal rights and species preservation. All problems must be seen to have global, national and local characteristics and the marketing strategy must identify with the issues at each of these levels. Perspective must be backed up with commitment. Such commitment must recognise the need to translate marketing rhetoric into reality in a proactive way. Thus such a green marketing approach must be consistent with the aims and strategies of environmental management techniques including the introduction of an environmental policy, an environmental improvement programme and environmental education.

However, in keeping with the arguments laid out in earlier chapters of this book we must therefore argue that traditional approaches to green marketing are less likely to be compatible with the techniques of ecological management and the strategies required to bring about a sustainable future. A new approach which takes these issues on board within an ethical framework

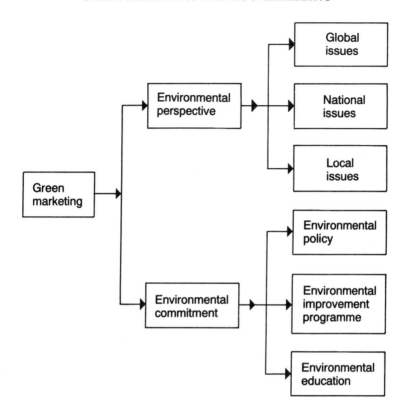

*Figure 7.1* Elements of the green marketing strategy

represents the leap forward which green marketing really ought to reflect.

## ECOLOGICAL APPROACHES TO GREEN MARKETING

We have argued that green marketing ought to represent a discrete shift in emphasis away from traditional approaches which put stress on certain aspects of a product towards an ethical approach which takes a holistic view of the product from cradle to grave and considers the context in which it is produced. Green marketing is about the provision of information about the product and the manufacturer to the consumer along with advice on how to use the product most successfully and advice on the re-use, repair, recycleability and disposal of the product. It therefore represents product stewardship at its best. It aims not only to meet the needs of the consumer but considers all stakeholders. It is not only about selling, but encompasses wider issues such as environmental education and campaigning for the issues which will help bring about sustainability.

The stakeholder concept emphasises the need to satisfy a whole range of often disparate demands and the role of green marketing is to track these demands and to try to satisfy them where appropriate. For example, there will be demands from customers for environmentally friendly products at reasonable prices with high quality attributes, demands from shareholders for profitability and dividends, and demands from employees for fair wages and job security. Where conflict between competing aims exist it has been the stakeholders with most power (usually measured in crude financial terms) who win the battle. However, if our ultimate aim is sustainable development all other demands must be considered as secondary to this and profit-centred strategies replaced by more holistic and integrated approaches. A starting point must be to make stakeholders aware of each other's demands in an open and honest way. This approach, which has been alien to so many organisations in the past, must be part of an organisation's corporate culture if the company is to claim honestly that it is seeking to improve the whole of its environmental performance.

The most important lesson to be learned from the stakeholder concept is that cooperation is as important as competition. Trust relations have to be developed with stakeholders and this is best built up by honesty and openness. Companies who are serious about improving their environmental performance should have nothing to hide and therefore the disclosure of as much information as possible, without giving away competitive advantages, is central to a sustainable strategy.

Although environmental considerations are increasingly important to the consumer, environmental attributes alone will be insufficient to sell a product. Not only must the product recognise traditional market requirements (i.e. it must be fit for the purpose for which it was intended, have the desired quality and delivery attributes and be price competitive), it must also consider its profile and the profile of its producer with regard to wider ecological issues such as worker rights, the treatment of women and minority groups, animal testing and any impact on the Third World and indigenous populations. Failure to meet these basic requirements will ultimately result in failure of the product.

Green marketing cannot be looked at in isolation. The effects of launching a new product or re-orienting an existing one to have superior environmental attributes will have ramifications for procurement, finance, human resources, production processes and delivery. As we have advocated throughout this book, the fundamental key to a green marketing strategy is to approach the problem in a systemic way, undertaking thorough research and planning. Consideration of longer timescales for activities will also be important.

The logistics by which a company improves its environmental performance will depend in part on its functional organisation, its geographical spread and its markets. Ultimately though, the organisation must make the environment a priority. Within the marketing mix there are a number of priorities which need to be addressed, as identified in the following checklist:

1 Corporate policy: green marketing is as much about marketing the organisation as any of its products. It is no good producing a product with superior environmental attributes if the very nature of the firm in which it is produced leads to severe ecological degradation. There is therefore a need to ensure that the organisation has in place appropriate ecological management strategies and that it is committed to moving towards sustainability.

2 Product policy: products should be designed with sustainability in mind. In particular they should minimise the use of non-renewable resources and be designed for dis-assembly and recyclability. Products with clear environmental attributes can be labelled as such but it is important not to overstate or be dishonest about the environmental aspects of the product. More importantly, a product stewardship approach should accompany the sale of the product ensuring that the customer uses the product as it is intended.

3 Packaging: packaging should be designed which, whilst fit for its purpose, uses the minimum amount of materials. Use should be made of packaging materials which do less damage to the environment and the company should arrange for packaging to be recycled or taken back and where possible re-used. Excess

packaging used as promotional material is unethical and not in the spirit of sustainability.

4 Promotion policy: promotions should highlight the environmental credentials of both the organisation and its products or services. The environmental reputation of the firm may be enhanced by public relations and advertising exercises but all claims must be credible, honest and true. Moreover, promotions should merge with education and campaigning (see below) so that organisations are involved in broadly based strategies to improve the environment and to move towards sustainable development.

5 Pricing policy: if environmental measures cost extra money then this can be passed on to the consumer making it clear that the price differential is a result of environmental improvements. If costs are reduced through environmental measures then it is ethical to be completely honest in cutting prices or considering discounts to those who can match the organisation's own environmental performance.

6 Transportation and distribution: preference should be given to transportation systems which have reduced environmental costs in terms of energy consumption and pollution (widely defined). Where appropriate, distribution channels should be established between the producer, wholesalers, retailers and customers which minimise transportation and packaging needs. These same systems can also be used to ensure that used products and packaging can be recycled.

7 Quality and effectiveness: quality is part of the environmental profile of a product. Quality goods last longer, break down less frequently, are worth repairing and often use less energy in their use. It is important that any environmental attributes do not detract from quality or the effectiveness of the product. If this is not possible then that fact should be clearly explained to the consumer. Ecological management requires a move away from quantity and towards quality.

8 Personnel policy: commitment is at the heart of a proactive strategy for sustainable development and it is important to ensure that the whole workforce is sensitive to environmental issues and understands how to ensure environmental improvement. Awareness of the importance of the environment should be enhanced by training and education and there should be

employee reward schemes which improve the environmental performance of the organisation.

9 Environmental information systems: the organisation must ensure that there is an adequate environmental monitoring system which is capable of identifying potential and real problems. Suppliers must be made aware of corporate requirements and must have their own strategies which are consistent with the organisation's environmental policy. The organisation must collect and collate relevant information so that it can be responsive to stakeholders.

10 Education, communications and product stewardship: linked closely with environmental information systems there must be a clear strategy for communications with consumers, which will include education about the product they are using and how to use it more effectively, advice on what to do after the product has been used and an element of wider education and campaigning in the context of sustainable development.

Whilst the ten elements of a green marketing strategy outlined above will move the organisation towards a more sustainable strategy it must be remembered that the marketing function does not exist in isolation and that no positive environmental claims can be made unless the whole organisation is functioning along the lines identified in the first six chapters of this book. Fundamental to the green marketing function will be the collection and management of information and a clear communications role. These are issues which we need to deal with in rather more depth.

## ENVIRONMENTAL INFORMATION

Central to any green marketing strategy will be the identification of new issues, market trends and the state of scientific knowledge and technology. Market research and accurate information will be needed on which to build successful campaigns. Marketing requires information to be effective and therefore greener marketing is nothing without accurate information on the environmental impact of both the company and its competitors. A continuous flow of information and data is needed on both processes and products and central to this will be life cycle analysis, environmental audits and environmental impact assessment. At least the first two of these should be on-going activities. On top of this there is a need for information relating to the overall performance and environmental conduct of the whole organisation. However, information is often collected in a rather haphazard sort of way and this leads to a narrow and piecemeal focus. There is therefore a need for some sort of environmental information system where information is collected and collated in a planned and productive way. The aim of such a system must be to enable managers to make more effective decisions and to act as a database for answering queries from stakeholders.

The first consideration is where to find relevant information. Here it is useful to group sources into three categories: primary sources, secondary sources and cooperative alliances. Let us deal with each in turn:

- Primary sources: primary information is very much about direct research. It means collecting information based on surveys of one sort or another. Large quantitative surveys based on questionnaires can elicit interesting information about overall market trend and changing consumer attitudes. Just as valuable, however, are more qualitative techniques associated, for example, with focus groups. Focus groups will often be useful in testing the results of large surveys. For example, we know that quantitative research suffers from the so-called halo effect, i.e., many interviewees want to appear more virtuous than they actually are. A more informal approach to the collection of data through the focus group can often elicit more truthful information.

- Secondary sources: secondary materials include trade and industry association publications, specialist journals and magazines in the environmental area, specialist consumer magazines, professional association materials, annual books and reviews, and specialist market surveys. These secondary sources are relatively cheap although they do not of course provide the specific focus which an individual firm may require. They do however create a useful reference library and provide general information on market trend and attitudes. Market studies, in particular, however, often provide a lot of very detailed research and sometimes produce forecasts of market and consumer trends. More market studies with a green focus are likely to be published as demand for them grows amongst businesses.

- Cooperative alliances: an important, often overlooked, means of gathering information is through cooperative alliances with other organisations. Alliances with other firms to collect general information will be more cost effective but even wider alliances can prove very useful. Arrangements with local pressure groups, universities, government agencies and non-governmental organisations (NGOs) can all provide marketing managers with extra eyes and ears and different perspectives on environmental information. It is possible to establish think-tanks made up of groups of people with diverse interests and specialisms and this will often provide an in-depth, unbiased approach to public policy research which is simply not possible using any other source. The outcomes of these sorts of exercises (often used in association with primary and secondary research) are often of extremely high quality.

We can also consider environmental information as broadly falling into three categories when we wish to consider some sort of typology. Figure 7.2 maps out an environmental information system where we have categorised information into stakeholder information, impact information and scientific information. This all feeds into a central data collection function and library. Let use deal with each type of information in turn.

- Stakeholder information: we know from earlier chapters of this book that one of the challenges facing the modern environmentally aware enterprise is to satisfy the many (often disparate) wants of a whole range of stakeholders. It is therefore important to monitor these wants through systems which collect information from employees, customers, shareholders, local communities and others. Each of these stakeholders brings a different dimension to the organisation. The organisation's environmental policy and stakeholders' reactions to that and the associated environmental management system will be one strand which pulls together information. Other information is likely to be more primary information about consumer attitudes, pressure group activities and regulators' reactions.
- Impact information: central to any open, honest and credible marketing policy will be a need to understand and have information about the environmental impact of the organisation's operations and processes. Again there will be two distinct streams of information. On a continuous basis there should be monitoring of all inputs to the organisation and all outputs (including discharges, emissions and other pollution) from the

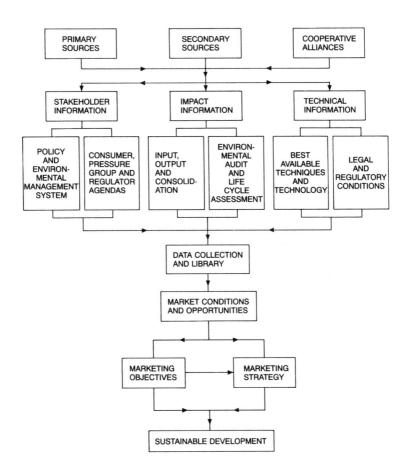

*Figure 7.2* Environmental information system

organisation. There should be a periodic consolidation to check that there are no hidden wastes or discharges. Secondly, the marketing function should be able to draw on periodic audit reports and full life cycle assessments of all its products. Life cycle assessment, in particular, will be central to any green marketing campaign.

- Technical information: technical issues play a prominent role in virtually every aspect of the organisation's environmental strategy. It is important, for example, to have knowledge of best available techniques and best available technologies since in most countries this is required by law either implicitly or explicitly. Secondly, to be proactive there is a need to collect information on the legal and regulatory environment both as it stands at one point in time and as part of a forward planning exercise.

We can see from Figure 7.2 that all this information, held together in a reference library should give us a picture of market conditions and opportunities and will be used to formulate marketing objectives and a marketing strategy. Ultimately those objectives and that strategy should be consistent with the aims of sustainable development through ecological management techniques and strategies consistent with sustainability.

## COMMUNICATIONS

Communications will be a key element in any marketing process. Accurate information about products and wider environmental aspects of processes should be communicated to all stakeholders and particularly customers. In particular, at the centre of the green marketing process should be a product stewardship approach where advice and help about the use and disposal of the product should be given to all those who will come into contact with it after it has left the factory gates. There is, of course, no magic green method or style of promotion and information provision. Essentially explaining the attributes of an environmentally friendlier product should be approached in just the same way as any other communication message. The central message should always be visible, understood, relevant, and honest. The company should be prepared to prove what has been said and be open to further questions about its overall environmental profile.

Companies which are promoting an environmentally friendly

image will have to be very precise about what they say and truly practise what they preach. Drawing attention to the environmental aspects of a business will increasingly draw attention from a more sceptical public and better-informed media. If there is something about a product or organisation worth communicating then the key question must be: to whom do you communicate? Undoubtedly the first group to concentrate on is the consumers of the product.

However, the green message may be rather more difficult to communicate than many consumer surveys of green attitudes might suggest. We have already argued that the halo effect promotes rhetoric and obscures reality. Whilst theoretically willing to buy alternative products, we know that most consumers are not, in practice, happy about giving up the brands they know and the price, quality and performance standards they have come to expect, especially for alternative, more uncertain purchases which might actually be at a higher price. One of the problems is that past marketing campaigns with respect to greener products have made situations worse by being deceitful. Many consumers have become confused, cynical and disillusioned with many greener products. Companies cannot therefore jump to conclusions about consumers' understanding of, and likelihood to respond to, greener communications. There is a need to look very closely at markets and consumer behaviour before effective communications can be developed. In the main, the onus will be on the marketeers to educate consumers, simplify environmental issues and then offer product solutions.

The consumer will also be affected indirectly through the behaviour of competitors and through the media, politicians and environmental pressure groups. There are therefore many other key targets for any greener communications. Increasingly, business-to-business communication is becoming more and more important for manufacturers and suppliers. If a company (and particularly a retailer) is developing its environmental stance, they are going to be more demanding of the environmental practices of their suppliers.

As discussed above, the first consideration concerning green communication is often not what to say about your company or product, but whether there is anything to say at all. There are two concerns here. Firstly, communicating a less-than-thorough or dubious environmental initiative runs the risk of alienating consumers and opinion formers if there are gaps in the message, inaccuracies in the claims or secrets in the organisation. In overstating environmental claims, negative regulatory, pressure group and media responses could endanger the product, service or corporate integrity. Bad publicity could negate everything which the company was trying to achieve and would certainly act against any positive corporate image which a company was trying to foster. Secondly, there is an issue concerning whether a green message is appropriate to consumers at all. The impact of the message will depend on how aware, committed and educated the consumers of a product are and on the particular market characteristics in which the product is sold. In the first instance a company needs to establish whether environmental considerations are or could be significant in their markets, and whether appropriate messages could confer a competitive advantage.

There are a number of communications techniques which can be used to get the message across. However, in order to be effective it is important that, whichever methods are chosen, they are used within an integrated and coordinated environmental strategy, consistent with other aspects of the company's environmental strategy. Even now, consumers are still swamped with the clichéd, generic imagery of greening in environmental messages: rainbows, trees, plants, green fields, dolphins, and smiley planets. These images have been used over and over again and as a result, consumers have tended to remember generic product categories, such as environmentally friendly detergents, rather than particular brands. At the other end of the scale far too many messages have assumed detailed consumer knowledge across the range of environmental issues. There is a need to explain each issue where appropriate and then stress the reason why the consumer should prefer one particular product over its competitors' products.

In terms of executing communication, companies should not overestimate people's knowledge or altruism when it comes to any green issues. Neither should they underestimate how much consumers like their current brands. The majority of consumers will not be impressed with complicated explanations of why one product is more environmentally friendly than another. Those communicating the difference need to find simple and honest messages about why one product should be preferred.

Communications through the medium of advertising is likely to form part of any green marketing strategy. However, we have already suggested that clichéd imagery and stereotypical role models are hardly consistent with a move towards sustainable strategies. Sexist, racist and homophobic categorisations of people are more likely to cause offence to educated consumers than convince them to buy a particular product or service. Moreover, the tokenism paid to minority groups which is apparent in many commercials is equally offensive and will be interpreted as a cynical attempt to appear ethical. Indeed images of people in any situation are likely to be open to criticism.

It is often clear what should be avoided in advertising campaigns but less clear what is effective and consistent with sustainable strategies. Callenbach *et al.* (1993) suggest five aspects which product advertising should stress:

- lasting rather than transient buyer satisfaction;
- lifetime costs of products rather than just initial costs;
- reliability, durability and trouble-free qualities rather than initial emotional attractiveness;
- possibilities for the re-use or recycling of products and their containers; and
- the low ecological-impact features of the manufacture, distribution, use and disposal of the products.

Communicating the ethical, ecological and sustainable message will be very much part of a holistic strategy. Great care has to be taken about that communications strategy, particularly with respect to advertising. Like all ecological strategies, however, the key is to be honest, open and credible and to develop a communications strategy which is consistent with all the other aspects of corporate planning and management.

## ECO-LABELLING

Over time, eco-labelling schemes have been devised in a number of countries in an attempt to promote the use of production methods which are less harmful to the environment. The first such scheme was introduced in the Federal Republic of Germany in 1978. Canada, Japan and Norway established their own schemes in 1989. The European Union's eco-labelling scheme saw its first labels applied to washing machines in 1993.

Such schemes attempt to provide an independent recognition of the positive environmental profile of an individual product. It is

important therefore that product labelling ensures that products
and product groups are examined in a comprehensive way, usually
based on a life cycle assessment (see chapter 5), and where appropriate provide a measure of the effectiveness and safety of a product. However, not all labels appearing on goods are third-party
accredited and this has led to confusion and a considerable degree
of cynicism on the part of consumers.

The US Environmental Protection Agency (EPA, 1993) identifies
the environmental labelling of products as falling into categories
based on the following three key attributes. Firstly, all labelling
programmes which are independent of manufacturers and sellers
can be considered as 'third party' rather than 'first party' environmental claims. Secondly, participation in these schemes can be seen
as voluntary or mandatory. Thirdly, labelling programmes can be
positive, negative or neutral; that is, they can promote positive
attributes of products, they can require disclosure of information
that is inherently neither good nor bad, or they can require information on negative aspects of a product by, for example, providing
warnings about the hazards of products. Table 7.1 illustrates five
types of environmental labelling programmes using these criteria.

Table 7.1 Comparison of environmental labelling methods

| Label type | Positive | Neutral | Negative | Voluntary | Mandatory |
|---|---|---|---|---|---|
| 1 Seal-of-approval | ✓ | | | ✓ | |
| 2 Single attribute certification | ✓ | | | ✓ | |
| 3 Reports | | ✓ | | ✓ | |
| 4 Information disclosure | | ✓ | | | ✓ |
| 5 Hazard warnings | | | ✓ | | ✓ |

Seal-of-approval programmes identify products or services as
being less harmful to the environment than similar products or
services with the same function. Early seal-of-approval labels were
commonly awarded by large retail chains and national independent
third party schemes have grown out of this. Single attribute certification programmes typically indicate that an independent third

party has validated a particular aspect of the product and allows that to be used as a single issue environmental claim. Once again, however, this has led to some confusion with marketers labelling goods as 'environmentally friendly' based on this single issue. Such an approach is clearly unethical. Reports tend to offer consumers neutral information about a product and/or a company's environmental performance in multiple impact categories (e.g. energy consumption, water pollution). Consumers are therefore left to consider for themselves what they consider to be the most important environmental impacts. Information disclosure labels are also neutral, disclosing facts about a product which would not otherwise be disclosed by the manufacturer. However, the distinction here is that information disclosure labels are required by law. Hazard warning labels are also required by law and contain mandatory warnings about a product's adverse environmental or health effects (e.g. cigarette warnings).

The last two labels in this category are mandatory and provide information which is wider than positive environmental claims. Because of their voluntary nature, on the other hand, the first three categories can be seen together as environmental certification programmes (ECPs). ECPs are viewed by many governments as one of the policy tools which can be used to achieve environmental policy goals. According to the US EPA (1993) several studies have shown that ECPs may significantly influence consumers' purchasing decisions, allowing governments to further their environmental agendas. However, the success of market-driven environmental initiatives depends to a large extent on consumer awareness and knowledge of environmental issues. To use the market effectively as an environmental policy tool, there must be some assurance that environmental claims made on products are truthful and result in real environmental quality improvements. Furthermore such activity should be linked to national environmental policy goals as well as consumer concerns. When consumers are misled by trivial or false advertising, environmental policy goals driven by those concerns are undermined. The effectiveness of environmental marketing activities as policy tools therefore need to be ensured through several means: industry regulation (voluntary and mandatory), government intervention in the design and use of products, and third party certification of products.

Given the experience of environmental labelling in the past and problems associated with spurious and misleading claims, ethical businesses will always seek third party verification of any claim they are making or any label which they wish to use. Third party consumer product labelling can serve three functions in the marketplace. Firstly, it can act as an independent evaluation and endorsement of a product. Secondly, it can operate as a consumer protection tool and, thirdly, it can be used to achieve specific policy goals set by either the firm itself or regulatory agencies. As an independent endorsement of a product, a label which is third party verified can offer companies a selling point which is more credible then any first party claims that they might make. For consumer protection, recognised third party labels provide security that the product they are buying will make a difference to the environment and not simply line the pockets of unethical enterprises. All third party product labels assume that better information will enable consumers to make more informed purchasing decisions. ECPs operate on the assumption that information on the environmental impacts of products tends to be more complicated than other kinds of product information, and that, in order to make purchasing decisions based on environmental considerations, consumers are in need of a clearly reported expert analysis of those impacts.

In addition to guiding consumer behaviour, an ECP can provide a clear incentive for manufacturers to change to less harmful materials and production processes. In theory, if the market shares of products certified by ECPs increase, manufacturers of products that did not receive or seek the label will be induced to change or risk losing market share. Those manufacturers of products without a label may seek to qualify for the ECP's label, thereby reducing their adverse environmental impacts. Alternatively, they may try to differentiate their products on another basis, such as lower price or higher quality. To encourage continual technological and environmental improvements it is important that ECPs continuously raise the standards for an award so that only a selected minority of products on the market meet the programme's requirements.

## SEAL-OF-APPROVAL PROGRAMMES

The focus of the approach taken in this book is to argue that companies need to take holistic, systemic and ethical approaches to their environmental strategies. Piecemeal approaches are seen as inadequate. In line with this, we must recognise that the most powerful and most useful of the approaches to eco-labelling must be that of third party seals of approval. These programmes award the use of a logo to products judged to be less environmentally harmful than comparable products, based on a specified set of criteria.

Virtually all seal-of-approval programmes which exist world-wide follow the same process, with some minor variations. Firstly, product categories are chosen and some form of life cycle assessment is undertaken. This determines the points in the product's life cycle where the most significant impact occurs. Award criteria for that product group are then set to reduce those impacts considered to be the most important or relevant. Manufacturers are then invited to submit products for assessment and the product will have to show significant environmental improvements over competitors in those particular areas, for the award of the label. As we shall see below, national programmes do, however, vary widely in the rigour of their quantitative analysis.

The United Nations (UNEP, 1991) has outlined what it considers to be the essential points of a seal-of-approval programme as:

- determination of award criteria based on life cycle review of a product category;
- voluntary participation of potential licensees;
- run by a not-for-profit organisation, including governments, without commercial interests;
- recommendations for product categories and environmental award criteria determined by an independent, broadly based board;
- a legally protected symbol or logo;
- open access to potential licensees from all countries;
- endorsement from government;
- award criteria levels established to encourage the development of products and services that are significantly less damaging to the environment; and;
- periodic review and, if necessary, update of both environmental award criteria and categories, taking into account technological and marketplace developments.

A significant debate surrounds which categories of products should be considered appropriate for an eco-label. The issues are most clearly demonstrated with reference to the motor car. There are those who would argue that to have an eco-label category for cars would mean that manufacturers would make extra efforts to reduce the environmental impact of their products and that environmental attributes would become increasingly important in the characteristics which make cars appeal to customers. On the other hand there are those who argue that to award an eco-label to a product which causes as much environmental degradation as the car would be to devalue the whole of the eco-labelling approach. The definition of product categories is therefore a key issue for the future.

Precisely how product categories are defined does vary widely between the national schemes in operation. The procedure for selecting product categories ranges from extensive research to determine the potential benefits of a new product category, to the selection of a product category based on loose guiding principles. The European Union's attempts at product assessment have been the most ambitious of any programme. Product categories are decided upon by the Commission and assigned to a 'lead country' for evaluation and standards setting. This process is based on original research to gather environmental information on product categories. Whilst this strategy provides for a very thorough analysis, the time taken to move to the award of labels to products has been very long and has led to some criticism.

Canada's Environmental Choice Programme does not perform original research to determine the environmental impact of products. Guidelines are established by a review of currently available life cycle information which is then reviewed by external consultants and technical experts in the environment ministry. In Japan the EcoMark programme takes a rather different approach. EcoMark follows 'guiding principles' in its selection of product categories, its development of award criteria, and in the awarding of its labels. These eight guiding principles are as follows:

- products incur a minimal environmental burden when used;
- products improve the environment (through reduced pollution) when used;
- products incur a minimal environmental burden when discarded after use;
- products contribute to environmental preservation in other ways;
- appropriate environmental pollution control measures are provided at the stage of production;
- energy or resources can be conserved with use of the product;

- products comply with laws, standards and regulations pertaining to quality and safety; and
- price is not extraordinarily higher than that of comparable products.

The EcoMark committee, with advice from experts, simply decides on the basis of the 'guiding principles' whether to approve a product category. Although this is seen as a somewhat piecemeal approach which runs the danger of allowing product categories because of positive attributes in one area whilst damage may still occur in another, its success is seen in the programme's award of eco-labels to 1800 products in 47 product categories in its first three years of operation alone.

There is also considerable debate surrounding exactly what criteria should be used to decide on the award of an eco-label. In general, standards are set so that only a few products in a category can meet them. The idea is to provide incentives for manufacturers making products in that category to improve their products to meet the award criteria. When the percentage of products within a product category receiving labels increases, standards can be raised to limit the number of awards. In this way, a programme can provide an incentive for continuous improvement.

However, there has often been disagreement over, firstly, the weight given to certain environmental criteria, and secondly, what exactly constitutes an environmental impact. Where a full life cycle assessment has been performed, it is easier to spell out the precise areas of environmental impact on which criteria should concentrate. Although we know from chapter 5 that life cycle assessment is often problematic it seems nevertheless that disagreement over this first issue can be resolved through research. However, the second problem is more fundamental. We know from previous discussions in this book that we can view environmental issues in a number of ways. We have made clear distinctions, for example, between strategies associated with environmental management, ecological management and sustainable development. An eco-labelling scheme which was consistent with environmental strategies would therefore take a much narrower view of what constitutes a problem than if we took the wider worldview encapsulated in the concept of sustainable development. A wider view of what constituted an important factor implicit in the approach of sustainable development would include, for example, animal rights and the rights of indigenous populations in the Third World.

Such human and animal rights have long been a part of a wider ecological dimension which we are advocating in this book. A pragmatic position would be that ecological ethics should embrace all sentient beings (Wheeler, 1993b). Thus humans, whales, elephants and laboratory animals are clearly part of the moral community. In contrast, bacteria and tsetse flies are not. Therefore criteria for the award of an eco-label should, as a minimum, include consideration of the impact on animals and in particular, not allow animal testing as a base criterion. This is an approach which would be consistent with political and social reality and the views of consumers. A variety of public opinion polls and other sources of information may be cited in support of this position. Thus eco-labels which ignore the wider issues of human and animal rights, endangered species, biodiversity and the precautionary principle will be incomplete and flawed. They may be labels but they certainly will not be eco-labels (Wheeler, 1993b). Virtually no account has been taken of these wider issues in current eco-labelling programmes, however.

## THE EFFECTIVENESS OF ECO-LABELS

Environmental certification programmes (ECPs) are undoubtedly growing in popularity witnessed by their increasing use in a number of countries. However, it is less clear precisely how effective they actually are. One way to measure the effectiveness of an ECP must be based on the extent to which it meets its current objectives. According to the United States Environmental Protection Agency (EPA, 1993) all ECPs have approximately the same goals:

1 To circumvent misleading and false environmental advertising by providing an expert, objective assessment of the relative environmental benefits of the product;

2 To raise the awareness of consumers and to encourage them to take environmental considerations into account when making purchasing decisions;

3 To provide a market-based incentive to manufacturers to develop new products and processes that are less harmful to the environment; and,

171

4 To cause market changes that ultimately result in decreased environmental impacts from consumer products.

Attainment of this last goal would seem to be the ultimate measure of an eco-label's effectiveness. In theory, therefore, we should assess the environmental benefit gained from the eco-label programme implementation. However, this is a very difficult task and there is little available research evidence in this area. Programmes have therefore tended to measure secondary indicators of effectiveness that are more easily quantified, such as changes in product design and formulation, the market share of eco-labelled products and consumer awareness of the programme.

There have been several consumer surveys that measured issues such as logo recognition and most of these show a good deal of understanding after a clear advertising campaign has been undertaken by the authority awarding the labels. Whether that label then influences the consumer's purchasing decisions is rather less clear. On other measures, research is incomplete and it is rather early to tell if they will make a real difference to the operation of firms. In part, firms will make more changes if consumers recognise the labels and then use their existence to influence their purchasing decisions. Thus from the businesses' point of view, an ECP's effectiveness will be measured as a function of its benefits to producers and its related ability to change their environmental strategies. It should be stressed, however, that leading firms will not wait to see if eco-labels are a success but will put into place appropriate strategies for sustainable development irrespective of the existence of an ECP. Where appropriate, those firms will help to educate the consumer about the third party eco-labels and will ensure that those labels are awarded on appropriate and wide-ranging ecological criteria.

## CONCLUSION

Green marketing will be central to any business organisation committed to environmental improvement. However, it must be recognised that ethical and sustainable approaches must be central to the communications function. Moreover, green marketing is more than simply about selling products, it is also about educating the consumer about better use of a product in environmental terms and it is about being part of a wider campaign to move business towards sustainable development. It therefore represents a discrete shift away from the more unethical and spurious green marketing strategies so common to date. Key elements of the marketing strategy include the need to recognise and chart changing consumer trends, to have clear strategies aimed at differentiating the company's marketing mix and to have integrated and effective environmental information systems. It is not enough to promote products alone and any organisation needs to examine its overall impact on and commitment to the environment. The green company will also be a campaigning company and be committed to spreading an ethical communication message about sustainable development.

Companies which are keen to identify their more environmentally friendly products within their marketing strategy will also be aided by third party eco-labelling schemes, based on seals of approval, which will be able to confer a recognised accreditation for a particular product. As a minimum the assessment approach should be based on a full life cycle assessment of a product category and suitable minimum criteria laid down for the award of a label. However, the schemes which are in existence will have to take on wider ecological criteria including fundamental human and animal rights if they are to retain their credibility and really act as an effective tool to take us towards sustainable development. From the company's perspective it will not be enough to make minor changes to a product and call it environmentally friendly, since environmental impacts need to be assessed from cradle to grave. Increasingly consumers' attentions will be based on corporate performance as well as individual product profiles and therefore any strategy will have to focus on the widest possible aspects of environmental impacts. Companies who take the environment seriously need therefore to adopt a proactive green marketing strategy which is much more holistic than the narrower marketing so often employed by more traditional firms.

# 8

# REGIONALISM AND BIOREGIONALISM

## INTRODUCTION

The aim of this chapter is to begin to examine a structure of future society and of business organisation which would be compatible with the aims of sustainable development. Local action is the key to progress and we argue here that a new emphasis placed on regional development holds many of the keys to a sustainable future. Not least, organisation at the regional level is compatible with many of the principles of sustainable development outlined in Agenda 21. For example, Agenda 21 suggests that many of the problems and solutions associated with sustainable development have their roots in local activities, so local authorities have a key role to play. As the level of government closest to the people they have a role in consulting local communities and businesses; they can gather information with regard to the environment and build a consensus on sustainable development strategies.

The purpose of this chapter is therefore to identify sorts of initiatives which can be taken in the local economy which can not only improve regional environmental performance but, by involving businesses, can also aid the development of better environmental performance at the firm level. The chapter looks at two different approaches to the regional issue. The first is to examine the concept of the regional environmental management system (REMS) and the second is to advance the debate into the realms of deep ecology by outlining the important concept of bioregionalism. Both approaches are compatible and based upon the notion that there is a direct relationship between environmental quality and the industrial development and economic activities within an area or region, and that a key strategy for environmental management within businesses can be that of cooperating in order to achieve the integration of economic and environmental objectives. Bioregionalism, however, has huge implications for the sort of industrial organisation which exists into the future. It is argued that the large conglomerate organisation, controlled in a unitary fashion, is no longer sustainable, economically or environmentally, and that the future lies in the reorganisation of industry into post-Fordist networks.

## THE IMPORTANCE OF REGIONALISM

European Union environmental policies on land, water and air pollution have important consequences for planning and use of the Community's land area. In the EC's Europe 2000 project (Commission of the European Communities, 1991), the issue of the linkage between economic development and the environment is highlighted particularly because quality of life is becoming an important factor in the ability of regions and cities to attract new inward investment. There is a need therefore for regional development policies to reach the right balance between protection of the physical environment and economic growth. Once again, this requires a strategy at the regional level which links the interests of communities and businesses.

The definition of a region used here is a relatively small geographical area of a suitable size for a project to be undertaken to improve the environmental performance of that area. It might be a local authority's area of jurisdiction (although this is almost certainly too wide), a particular city or town or even part of a city which can be segregated. It might be an urban or rural area. However, most importantly, it needs to be of a such a size that the commitment of industry within the area can be channelled into action and it needs to be sufficiently small to allow every participant industry to feel important enough to make an effort towards environmental improvement.

The thing which links these possibly disparate regions is the method by which the environment of the region can be improved. The underlying approach of the regional environmental management system (REMS) is to develop a plan for the region which will, over time, lead to the development of a comparative advantage based on integrated environmental management, at both company and regional level. This is consistent with the approach of the EU's

Fifth Environmental Action Programme when it suggests that local and regional authorities can play a decisive role 'in creating the necessary conditions to enable individuals and private enterprises to play their respective roles' whilst ensuring 'the sustainable use of resources necessary for that development to take place and prosper' (Fleming, 1992: 4). Bioregionalism, however, goes further than that, arguing that ultimately each region must live within its natural limits to growth and that at the local level, social, economic and ecological factors are all synonymous.

Whatever the approach taken, the development of the region must be based on high environmental and product quality at every stage of the production process and at every step in the production chain which will be integrated as far as possible within the region. At the product level, an emphasis on 'cradle-to-grave' responsibility and integrated supply chains leads to an increased control of the production cycle from primary production right through to direct marketing and final sale. One specific aim will be to encourage different production steps to take place within the same region. This would include the key objective of dealing with the disposal and treatment of waste within the region in which it was created. New opportunities for economic development may therefore arise in the region.

Although the approaches of the regional environmental management system (REMS) and bioregionalism are compatible they are nevertheless divided by ideology. The REMS approach is about taking what is here and now and redesigning systems to merge environmental considerations with economic considerations at the level of the organisation and the region. It is therefore about reform and consistent with modern approaches to environmental management. Bioregionalism, on the other hand, is about more radical structural change, challenging the very foundations of both the modern industrial enterprise and placing the region firmly within its own ecological boundaries. We might consider this approach as running parallel to the approach of ecological management with its philosophy grounded in deep ecology. However, the two approaches should not necessarily be seen as separate and distinct. Traditional environmental management techniques provide a road down which we should tread, but then challenge us to go further in adopting more ecological principles. In stressing the role of the region, and of development within that region, the regional environmental management system approach naturally leads us on to a consideration of bioregionalism, in a similar way. We must see the REMS approach as similar to BS7750. Neither can guarantee us sustainable development, but both take us off in the right direction as a starting point. The debate, once again, centres on the differences in approach between environmental strategies, ecological strategies and strategies consistent with sustainable development.

## THE REGIONAL ENVIRONMENTAL MANAGEMENT SYSTEM (REMS)

We have argued throughout this book that we must not treat economic forces and the environment as if they were separate and non-interacting elements. This is exemplified in so many regions where single-minded economic development has resulted in the exploitation of the natural environment, leaving rivers biologically dead and parts of the landscape aesthetically degraded and sometimes contaminated. The common approach taken for dealing with this problem is that taken by traditional neo-classical economists, who argue that an economic value should be placed on natural assets and that these costs can then be internalised by the institution causing the damage (see, for example, Pearce and Turner, 1990). Conceptually, there seems to be no quarrel with the fact that long term economic benefits accrue from environmental management. However, a significant tension between neo-classical economics and ecological management often arises around short term issues because of the difficulty of accurately valuing natural assets and problems associated with the ownership of those assets.

A full cost accounting option which would internalise all environmental costs remains speculative and highly controversial, and there are many ecologists and environmental managers who doubt both the wisdom and practicality of attempting to reconcile all ecological impacts with conventional financial indicators. It is not possible to make realistic financial estimates of the intrinsic value of numerous important ecological assets and secondly it is not possible to predict what value would be placed on these assets by future generations. It is therefore impossible to envisage all key indices of sustainability emerging from traditional economics or cost accountancy. Moreover, such an approach involves handing down policy from above and monitoring and implementing it at a distance. We need to look towards a more holistic approach which deals with problems where they occur and involves all economic agents in moving forward in a more cooperative way.

There is therefore a role to be played in the development of an integrated regional environmental management system (REMS) which is capable of exploring the synergistic effect of applying environmental management policies to all sectors of activity. This change from a somewhat piecemeal to a holistic approach can be seen as an important part of an approach consistent with sustainable development. The concept of sustainable development recognises that there is an interdependence between the economy and the environment, not only because the way we manage the economy has an impact on the environment, but also because environmental quality has an impact on the performance of the economy.

Central to the development of a REMS is the cooperation and commitment of regional and local resources facilitated through partnerships between individuals, businesses, public sector institutions and other agencies. A strategy of regional environmental management is required which promotes and stimulates community implemented development. It is particularly important therefore to involve the business sector and to make it clear that there are significant benefits to that sector becoming involved. This process must begin through the provision of information, through education and training, and subsequently the provision of support, advice, and capital for local initiatives. Any environmental management system starts with, and depends strongly upon, the development of understanding and commitment from all people involved and the REMS is no exception.

There is also a need to have a clear policy for the region which integrates both regional objectives and industrial aspirations. Such policies are already in place where local authorities have followed Friends of the Earth advice in introducing a declaration of commitment to environmental protection and policy development in the areas of recycling, energy, transport and planning, environmental protection and enhancement, health, and the monitoring and minimisation of pollution. Some authorities have also introduced regular environmental audits and invited public and industrial participation.

However, the regional environmental management system policy needs to go beyond this and fully integrate the needs of the region, industry and the public into a plan which binds them together with

178

the objective of significantly improving all aspects of the region's environmental performance.

## THE BENEFITS OF A REGIONAL ENVIRONMENTAL MANAGEMENT SYSTEM

Traditional approaches to regional management and regional planning often centre around environmental rehabilitation and prevention of further environmental degradation, through the introduction of specific management and control systems. The REMS concept goes further than that because it not only introduces environmental management on a regional scale, but actively uses it as a tool to enhance the economic prospects of the region by integrating environmental, economic and social factors in the REMS. Regional management involving such an integrated approach, whereby all developments and all economic activities are seen as part of a larger structure, will have a number of general beneficial effects.

A REMS development team, with representatives from local communities and industries, and local government will set environmental targets and protocols at all levels. Targets will be continuously re-assessed and every person in the community will have their own environmental responsibility. As a result of this integrated approach, different companies are more likely to cooperate in dealing with pollution and other environmental problems thereby potentially reducing costs. The Landskrona project in Sweden and the Prisma project in the Netherlands are well known examples which demonstrated that such a strategy can work, and that the environmental problems of companies, even if they operate in different industries, are often quite similar (Van Berkel et al., 1991).

Both the region as an entity, and the individual companies within that region, may benefit from an increased marketability. Possibilities exist for marketing the region as a whole bringing generic benefits to companies operating within it. It must be clear that the product comes from a region in which high threshold environmental criteria have been established. New investors may be attracted to the area, because of its more efficient management system. The landscape and countryside will be better managed and preserved. Increased environmental planning in the REMS could lead to innovative design and management and to an ecologically sound, socio-economic structure. In turn, a coordinated, cooperative and active approach to environmental rehabilitation can be undertaken, leading to a cleaner, healthier and safer environment. Moreover, a programme aimed at prevention of further environmental damage will integrate wider aspects of economic development and improve quality of life. The REMS is also likely to involve making the most of space, landscape, cultural and craft traditions, architectural and industrial heritage.

Most of the synergistic effects of the regional environmental management system will only occur if all parties involved not only understand the conversion concept, but are also willing to cooperate and actively strive towards its success. The main strength of the REMS lies in the integrative approach towards environmental, economic and social factors.

## IMPLEMENTATION STRATEGIES

The REMS approach stresses the voluntary approach implicit in traditional environmental management strategies and puts great emphasis on the role of an environmental management system in the region as well as within the organisations operating within that region. It is argued that the goals for economic development inherent in planning for the REMS will be achieved through the development of regional comparative advantage based on self-imposed market-led codes of practice that ensure quality and integrated environmental management (Welford, 1993). Both the company-based environmental management system and the REMS build a strategic link between business objectives and environmental pressures. The two can no longer be seen as separate and the particular objectives of businesses and environmental improvement have to be seen as not inconsistent, as has traditionally been the case. Moreover, the development of the REMS is deliberately in line with company-based environmental management system standards such as BS7750 and the eco-management and audit scheme.

The regional environmental management system requires a good source of up-to-date information about its starting point and its on-going performance. There is a need, as far as possible, to undertake an initial review of the region which will act as a benchmark for future measurement. Using the same sort of approach adopted by firms with environmental management systems there is subsequently a need to regularly audit environmental performance and the REMS itself.

Like the company-based environmental management system, the REMS should be regarded as a management tool, aimed at facilitating implementation of the regional conversion plan, and comparable to the function of the environmental management system at the company level. It should facilitate environmental rehabilitation and protection by integrating economic, social and environmental factors, emphasising local industry and local interests. Instrumental to the development of the REMS will be the planning team. Specific tasks for this team can be identified in the following ten point strategy:

1 Develop a regional environmental information system, including an environmental monitoring system.
2 Conduct an extensive environmental and socioeconomic study in the area, with emphasis on topics such as migration patterns, effects of infrastructural developments, employment, and the relative importance of the different economic sectors.
3 Extend contacts and communication with local communities and industry.
4 Develop internal strategies to promote information and education of all residents of the area towards environmental protection and the benefits and implications of the REMS and to stimulate community involvement and environmental awareness.
5 Design a template and model for processes and protocols within the area, resulting in improved communications and increased organisational control.
6 Outline a regional environmental policy, with specific standards and targets.
7 Conduct a detailed environmental quality survey to identify and prioritise areas for environmental rehabilitation and development.
8 Stimulate and coordinate further development and implementation of company environmental management systems.
9 Identify and prioritise areas for economic investment and growth, and to identify new economic opportunities.
10 Develop strategies to promote and market the area externally and to develop a scheme that gives recognition to 'green companies' within the region.

We know that environmental development can best be established when there is a sense of cooperation and commitment from all parties involved (see Welford, 1992). It is suggested, therefore, that for the development of a conversion plan, representatives of both local communities and industrial sectors are brought together in a development committee and not only help develop, but also ensure broad-based support for the final conversion plan.

The establishment of a company environmental management system is a relatively low cost exercise. The benefits of a company EMS have been outlined in detail by Welford (1992), and research in the USA, with its high environmental standards and stringent laws, showed that costs of pollution control add up to a mere average of 0.54 per cent of a company's overall costs (Dodwell, 1992). Total environmental expenditures are on average 2.4 per cent of turnover (Winsemius and Guntram, 1992). Over a period, instalment of a company EMS will pay for itself several times over. Therefore, expenditure to install company environmental management systems should have a short payback period and can be self-financing.

As far as the costs of the REMS are concerned these will depend on the amount of expertise, in the way of consultants, needed to be introduced into the region and the size of the project itself. Infrastructural investment is clearly required to address the issues of emissions and effluent management and rehabilitation but expenditure of this kind is likely to take place anyway. An additional benefit of the REMS is that such expenditure is likely to be done in a more integrated and systematic way. The initial review of the region may be costly but it is invaluable in identifying priorities for action. In many cases, however, local authorities have already started on the process and there are growing sources of regional environmental information.

Expenditure on the REMS needs to be seen as an investment good rather than a consumption good. It should be clear that any such investment will bring returns via improvements in the regional environment and new opportunities for businesses operating within that region. In turn, the increased wealth-generating potential in the region can mean that the project can ultimately pay for itself.

# BIOREGIONALISM

The essence of bioregionalism is to live as close to the land as possible, to decentralise organisations and to live in harmony with nature. Sale (1974) argues that a bioregion is part of the Earth's surface, the rough boundaries of which are determined by natural order rather than human dictates, distinguishable from other areas by attributes of flora, fauna, water, climate, soils and landforms, and the human settlements and cultures those attributes give rise to. He goes on to suggest that the borders between areas will not be rigid but they will be understood and sensed, or in some way known to the inhabitants, and particularly those rooted in the land. Thus the most fundamental form of bioregionalism parallels the traditional organisation of society which we have seen in the past in the North American Indians and at present in some indigenous populations of the Third World. Whilst a romantic dream to some, we argue here that some of the basic constructs of the bioregional model, interpreted in a more pragmatic way and translated through a postmodernist paradigm, offer us a development path consistent with sustainable development.

The bioregional model puts more emphasis on local activity, on local development and on the protection of the environment in a proactive way by all those living in certain areas. It stresses the importance of the local economy, of local employment and the development of local trading networks which are less reliant on traditional forms of mass transportation. The bioregional model also challenges the common acceptance of the need for large organisation, for large structures and for centralised government and institutions. It is a construct which bonds communities around the common purpose of environmental protection. But it is not a model which simply translates national cultural domination and suppression into regional control. Bioregionalism, properly conceived, not merely tolerates but thrives upon the diversities of human behaviour and implicitly increases the fundamental rights of those groups which are traditionally discriminated against.

Bioregionalism is open to interpretation. It is not a single model because the shape of bioregional society and the local economy will be shaped by those people within it rather than dictated by national and transnational organisations. It offers an image of the future that can be regarded as positive and liberating and realistic and energising. The question which we have to answer here relates to how businesses can change to be part of a move towards the bioregional model. The answer lies in considering what is actually happening within business at the moment. Indeed far from requiring a fundamental change in the way businesses operate, many would argue that the increasing decentralisation of business into post-Fordist cells is not inconsistent with the bioregional vision.

## THE POST-FORDIST ORGANISATION

The organisation sits between the political and the personal yet at the same time it is the political and the personal. If sustainability equates to the enhancement of the quality of life, the business organisation also has a role to play in the development of a technologically advanced economy unless we are to reject any material basis at all. In the current economic structure firms also have to look towards competitiveness. Yet there are tensions evident between the goals of competitiveness and sustainability which have to be resolved. Here, there needs to be a settlement, but that settlement will be different in every organisation.

Kohr (1957) claimed that economic decline was the result of no particular economic system but of size. If production units and markets are too big, then it would seem that economic goals ought to be towards decentralisation. Such decentralisation would seem to imply a redefinition of democracy with a new emphasis on local and organisational participation.

The environmental concerns about mass production and a trend away from production-line (often termed Fordist production) techniques in the workplace tend to point in the direction of smaller, more flexible firms and divisions. Although large firms will continue to exist, increasingly their production will be based on smaller scale production models with a significant increase in franchising and sub-contracting. Small scale units enable production to be specialised and to meet customers' requirements more accurately whilst modern production methods, often including new technological modes of operation, enable the unit to be flexible and responsive to changing demands.

There is a need to develop a flexible specialisation strategy in an environmentally friendly way. In purchasing new, clean technology, cost may not be the most important consideration and the firm needs to think carefully about multi-process technology which can produce an increased number of variations to a basic product. In addition it needs to look towards serving new and complementary markets and offering a high quality, personal service. The organisation and scheduling of production should enable a move away from batch processes wherever possible and working patterns need to be in line with levels of demand and not custom and practice. The workforce must become more flexible and specialised and there is a role for increased training and education.

The organisation must tread down new paths and deal with the uncertainty which that brings. Since the organisation is not much more than an amalgam of people it must take them with it and satisfy their desires and aspirations to a chosen extent. It must be flexible and responsive. Within the organisation there is therefore a renewed emphasis to be put on the concepts of self-determination, participation and cooperation. Sustainability is fundamentally linked to equality and equity and such an emphasis must start within the workplace.

## STRUCTURAL IMPLICATIONS OF BIOREGIONALISM

As the individual perspective leads on to the notion of the organisation of the firm, so the organisation of the firm forces us to consider the organisation of society. Notions of smaller scale organisation force us to look more at communities which make up that society. Indeed, the idea of community grows out of the people, their location and their shared experiences. A move towards a new emphasis on communities also leads us to question traditional forms of hierarchy. Natural hierarchy will be established through leaders who may be outside or inside the traditional political process. These are the central tenets of a decentralised bioregional development model which fits neatly inside a postmodernist perspective.

Bioregional economies must conserve resources and systems of the natural world and have a stable means of production and exchange. Within bioregions there must be cooperation and participation and growth must be seen as organic. Bioregionalism means living within the natural limits to growth. Moreover it stresses social and ecological processes as being one and inseparable. Thus there is a role for spatial reorganisation into small-scale communities (Sale, 1985) as the key to an ecological society.

Cosgrove (1990) argues that postmodernism recaptures many elements of pre-modern times, including a deep felt sense of moral order in nature and a unity with it. That is not to suggest that there is a need to go back to pre-industrial modes of living. However, bioregionalism's vision is similar to that of so-called eco-anarchists who advocate small-scale, decentralised commune-ism (Bahro, 1986), participatory democracy, a low growth economy, and non-hierarchical living. Such a model has become associated with the 'fourth world movement' encompassing activists living in communes or neighbourhood groups (particularly in the USA) and others who, via theory or practice, push the politics of regional or local separatism.

However, bioregionalism does not necessarily imply absolute separatism which can have xenophobic overtones. Regions and localities are nevertheless bound together, perhaps by a regional environmental management system or some other binding organisation (e.g. the law). This implies a single entity which puts stress on local development, local purchasing and production and a concerted move towards sustainability using all the alternative modes and methods which are of equal value within the postmodernist framework.

Some (e.g. Schwendtler, cited in Sarkar, 1983: 173) go further in arguing for a counter culture or 'alternative society'. This alternative milieu would include communes for production and distribution, residential communes, study circles, work groups, journals, health centres and free alternative schools and universities. At its most basic, however, we can identify three principles of bioregionalism:

1 Liberating the self, reducing the importance of impersonal market forces and bureaucracies, opening up local political and economic opportunities, enjoying communitarian values of cooperation, participation, reciprocity and confraternity, and having roots.
2 Developing the potential of a region towards self-reliance, emphasising small-scale, appropriate production, local markets and shared responsibility for sustainable development.
3 Understanding the value of the natural environment and living with it in a sustainable rather than an exploitative way.

Thus the bioregional paradigm differs hugely from the dominant vestiges of Modernism. It elevates the sense of oneself, ecological consciousness and a sense of place to a level more compatible with sustainable living. It stresses the very nature of a bioregion as any part of the Earth's surface whose rough boundaries are determined by natural characteristics or catchments (Kok *et al.*, 1993) rather than human dictates. This means that regional development can be promoted alongside industrial development and be managed according to sustainable principles (Welford 1993). Table 8.1 compares the traditional modernist constructs associated with the organisation of society, the economy and commerce with those of the bioregional vision. A move away from large scale to small scale is central to this comparison. The increased importance of cooperation, self-determination and self-sufficiency will be seen as a process of liberation to so many.

*Table 8.1* Bioregional constructs compared with modernist constructs

|  | Bioregional | Modernism |
|---|---|---|
| Industrial organisation | Flexible specialisation | Mass production |
|  | Economies of scope | Economies of scale |
|  | Self-determination | Managerial dominance |
|  | Cooperation | Hierarchy |
| Markets | Regional | National |
|  | Community-based | International |
|  | Specialised | Standardised |
| Economy aims | Conservation | Exploitation |
|  | Stability | Progress |
|  | Self-sufficiency | Global markets |
|  | Cooperation | Competition |
|  | Sustainability | Growth |
| Polity | Decentralisation | Centralisation |
|  | Consensus | Dominant ideologies |
|  | Diversity | Uniformity |
| Society | Symbiosis | Polarisation |
|  | Evolution | Directed development |
|  | Multi-cultural | Mono-cultural |

According to Sale (1985) communities based on bioregional principles have a number of other advantages as well. They would, for example, be insulated from boom and bust economic cycles, initiated from far away and being the product of distant economic control. They would be richer for not having to pay for imports or the financial and environmental costs of excessive transportation.

187

As identified by Ekins (1986) there would also be more appropriate trading relationships through the increased use of unofficial employment and trading exchanges.

The bioregional model will reduce society's alienation of the individual and of the small enterprise. More cohesion will mean more participation in the decisions of the community and regional cooperation will inevitably be encouraged by the needs of water and waste management and inter-regional transport and food distribution.

Thus although local, national and international markets will continue to exist, they will not occupy their present prominent position as the regulator of people's lives and the mechanism by which the industrial enterprise will live or die. Bioregionalism is about the reshaping of modern capitalism and the definition of a form of post-capitalism which stresses the role of cooperative institutions matched with local democratic frameworks and increased industrial democracy. Sustainable growth will occur only through indigenous resources and technology.

## CONCLUSION

It has been argued in this chapter that there are benefits relating to the introduction of some sort of regionalism, which integrates environmental, economic and social factors. A regional environmental management system approach can be a major step forward if it is developed by people that have an interest in the region, and central here is the participation, cooperation and commitment of businesses in the area. Coherent strategies and systems for environmental and developmental management, whether at the company level or at a regional level have synergetic benefits to businesses within it and to the local community and the environment. Changes in regional management must be designed and developed by people from within the region, supported by professional staff, and a central place in the management framework needs to be taken by representatives from local communities and industry. The role of local government is to provide linkage in the REMS.

Industry itself can benefit greatly by the additional help which will be provided by firms working together cooperatively with the support of a regional team. The REMS will complement the firm's own internal environmental management system and further add to the firm's competitive advantage if the region can attract a 'green label'. To a large extent the future of the environment and of the planet requires more cooperation and the concept of the regional environmental management system extends much of the best practice discussed by a wide range of practitioners. A key concept of environmentalists has long been associated with local action, global impact. At the centre of this concept is the need for increased cooperation and the REMS extends what firms alone can do towards achieving this important objective. However, we would argue that the REMS approach, whilst providing us with a road down which to tread, does not on its own deliver sustainability. There is a need to go beyond this approach and consider the concept of bioregionalism.

Bioregionalism is not a new concept but it has taken on a new role in the postmodern world and represents a vehicle for achieving sustainable development based on local organisation. There is the emergence of (for want of a better expression) New Times and these represent one way forward. Others may be possible, but they are not yet explainable or capable of being articulated. The acceptance of postmodernism offers a way forward through the legitimisation and recognition of new social movements and the abandonment of rigid structuralism.

The continuance of the present does little to move us towards a sustainable society. Reliance on voluntary codes of conduct and the new environmental standards heralded as our sustainable future hide the corporatist agendas which established them in the first place. Traditional capitalist society is covering over the cracks in the natural environment; it is not tackling the structural faults which put them there in the first place.

Far from presenting us with a generic model, the postmodernist perspective implicit in bioregionalism shows us that every organisation must move to try to control its own destiny. As it becomes more flexible and responsive it can reassess its own aims and objectives. It needs to take on the personal and the political. There is a role for the organisation to challenge and to educate and there is a central role here for communications technology and information management. The organisation needs to become empowered by empowering the people within it. New forms of organisation based on democratic, cooperative and collaborative principles are a possible way forward.

The environment is not a single challenge, its survival not dependent on one strategy. It stands alongside the other issues which capitalism subjugates. We need to move forward on all fronts or the gains made by one ideal may be at the expense of another. Bioregionalism provides a clear model for the direction in which we should move and is fully consistent with new modes of industrial organisation. The role of the modern industrial enterprise is no longer simply to be associated with the supply of goods. It will be a major agent in redefining the whole constructs of future societal organisation. However, before it takes on this role (which will move us swiftly to more sustainable modes of development) it must put aside the more popular ideologies of corporate environmentalism associated with unified action providing for 'business as usual'.

# 9

# TOWARDS THE TRANSCENDENT ORGANISATION[1]

## INTRODUCTION

It is the barriers imposed by modern society and the organisation of the economy which are the major barriers to environmental improvement worldwide. Short term profit-maximising strategies, an emphasis on materialism, the blind belief in the free market and free (international) trade, and deep-rooted individualism are all indicative of a society which is inherently unsustainable and heading for self-destruction. We must quickly improve the environmental performance of companies and countries to accord with the wider principles of sustainable development. This will mean challenging the very way in which we do business and, in turn, the way we organise industry.

Environmental performance is commonly reported in business literature as the organisation's record of achievement when compared with specific compliance or regulatory goals. It artificially treats the regulatory limits as an environmental target that an organisation should marginally exceed. Although these measures can be a practical and important element in achieving environmental performance they do not represent a consistent measure across jurisdictional areas. New environmental performance indicators are necessary that can combine these traditional approaches with more complex measures of satisfaction consistent with a postmodern era.

Traditional measurement of environmental performance usually reflects the organisation's external performance as a single identity. It is more appropriate to view an organisation as a group of components performing at different competency levels. Ecological performance measures should therefore reflect the internal

[1]The 'ROAST' scale used in this chapter was developed by John Dodge

191

environmental performance of each functional area of the organisation, its systems, strategies, structures, leadership and culture. Increasing integration of sustainable strategies into the existing internal workings of the organisation will be early indicators of future external environmental performance.

## ENVIRONMENTAL PERFORMANCE

Historically, business orientation was viewed as deeply rooted in the capitalist economy with the organisation acting in its own economic self-interest. The early performance measures reflecting the early accounting system would be profits, assets and liabilities. These measures become restrictive when the organisation is viewed as operating in a larger social system. We need to find measures of wider performance agendas which include social, ethical and ecological aspects.

In order to measure improving environmental performance we therefore need to define an ultimate goal towards which the organisation must move. This goal may not be achievable but it will serve as an upper boundary of sustainable performance on a five-point scale. Let us define this utopian form of organisation as the 'transcendent firm'. This firm will have ideals very similar to those of deep ecology and will perform in a way which is completely consistent with sustainable development. Although the debate on a definitive definition of deep ecology and its comparison to sustainable development is far from settled, for simplicity we consider the four pillars of the green philosophy and deep ecology to mix as one: ecology, grassroots democracy, social responsibility, and non-violence. It becomes quite obvious at this level of abstraction that human and animal rights, non-violent behaviour, ecological management and an emphasis on regionalism are all part of the same issue.

The least environmentally sensitive measure on our scale will be represented by the 'resistant organisation'. Thus the firm's environmental performance would be represented by extremely resistive behaviour. Organisations would totally disregard ecological issues in their decision making. The prime and ultimate motive of the organisation would be profit and the satisfaction of shareholders. The organisation would contain strong, pervasive, negative environmental values. It would tend to reject any green arguments as trite views of extremists and a few academics. Table 9.1 compares the extremes on our performance scale.

*Table 9.1* Environmental performance scale extremes

| *Resistant organisation* | *Transcendent organisation* |
| --- | --- |
| • Resists any green behaviour | • Internalises sustainable development |
| • Disregards green aspects in decisions | • Green criteria become paramount in decision making |
| • Willing to damage environment if beneficial to the organisation | • No decision of the firm will upset the ecological relationships |
| • Negative environmental values | • Environmental values take on an ideology associated with sustainable development |
| • Sees resources and nature for human profit and pleasure | • Human beings are not above nature but with nature; all decisions must reflect the intrinsic values and interrelationships of other members of the biosphere |
| • Resists any green intellectual or philosophical argument as trite views of extremists | |

We can further categorise an organisation's performance as lying somewhere between the resistant firm and the transcendent firm. A five point 'ROAST' scale would be represented by the following interval values:

| | | |
| --- | --- | --- |
| R | Resistance | Total resistance to environmental values and rules. Organisations would be |
| | Stage I | absolutely unresponsive and reactive to environmental initiatives. |
| O | Observe and comply | The organisation observes environmental laws but actions reflect an unwilling attitude or lack of ability to comply. |
| | Stage II | Actions are being enforced through legislation or court decisions. |
| A | Accommodate | Organisation begins to adapt to change. Early indications of proactive and responsive behaviours. Actions are no |
| | Stage III | longer based entirely on complying with environmental legislation but the organ- |

193

|   |   |   |
|---|---|---|
| | | isation begins to exhibit voluntary behaviour. |
| S | Seize and preempt | The organisation voluntarily seizes and preempts its actions with environmental concerns. It proactively engages in set- |
| | Stage IV | ting the agenda. It is responsive to the many external stakeholders. The latter phases would display the attributes of sustainable development. |
| T | Transcend | The organisation's environmental values, attitudes, beliefs and culture exhibit a total support for the environment. The |
| | Stage V | organisation would proactively support and be responsive to all living things. It would act in a way which is fully consistent with sustainable development. |

The ROAST scale can be useful in the classification of environmental performance responses from both external stakeholder groups and internal organisational functions, systems and activities. It integrates the deep ecology, social and business performance models of environmental performance. The scale, although it is a continuous spectrum, has been broken into five descriptive points for convenience. The extreme top-end of Stage V represents near-perfect environmental performance reflecting the near-theological views of deep ecology. The voluntary environmental actions of the organisation represented by Stages III and IV can be compared to the ideals of a more shallow ecology often typified in traditional approaches to environmental management. The organisation displays a proactive and responsive attitude and stance as it moves from accommodating the greening agenda to seizing and preempting it.

At level V the firm transcends traditional commercial performance measures and adopts strategies consistent with ecological management and sustainable development. It becomes almost evangelical in its green marketing strategy and considers very carefully whether it is operating at an appropriate scale.

## THE CONSUMER AND ENVIRONMENTAL
## PERFORMANCE

Dominant ideology from many free-market oriented governments suggest that it is the market which can act to improve an organisation's environmental performance. However, it is often simply assumed that individuals do display green behaviour. This is far from true and we can use our ROAST scale to categorise the environmental attitudes of consumers as well:

- Stage I consumers would purchase services or products without considering the environmental consequences. The sole criterion for purchase is to satisfy the needs of the consumer. No attention is paid to any environmental attributes of the purchase.
- Stage II consumers become more observant of environmental activities and reluctantly comply with existing laws. However, they display negative attitudes towards environmental legislation as restricting personal choice. Purchasing behaviour reflects only enforced actions.
- Stage III consumers begin voluntarily to seek out products that are less damaging to the environment. They are accommodative to environmental concerns.
- Stage IV consumers will question the need for the product as a legitimate use of the world's resources. A decision to purchase a product or service must meet the buyer's personal criteria for minimum environmental impact, resource- and energy-use. The purchasing behaviour would exhibit strong environmental demands of the manufacturer, focusing on impacts over the total product life cycle and its respect for humanity and other living things.
- Stage V consumers have strong values for all living things in the biosphere. Therefore all production and consumption must show deep respect for others in the ecosystem. This translates to a reduced level of human consumption to ensure that the eco-balance is maintained.

Thus as business moves forward on a sustainable agenda there is a need to take consumers along with it. A number of agencies including central and local government, non-governmental organisations and businesses all have a role to play. Business in particular, in integrating education and campaigning into its communications, will have to move consumers along the road toward sustainability

195

by producing more environmentally responsible goods and then convincing consumers of the need to purchase, use and dispose of these goods in an appropriate way. At the same time we should expect national government to introduce legislation incrementally which phases out the products which cause the most severe ecological damage and we should expect local authorities to introduce strong regional strategies which may include local purchasing policies.

Moving forward to sustainability is therefore a matter of partnerships at a number of different levels. At the root of those partnerships has to be a greater emphasis placed on cooperation. Businesses must play their full part and act as leaders in their markets rather than adopting compliance-based strategies or as followers of fashion. They should be the focus of education about particular products and processes and campaigns for the achievement of all the individual issues which together will build a future based on sustainable development.

## THE POLITICS OF ENVIRONMENTALISM

It would be an incomplete consideration of environmental issues which did not provide at least a cursory consideration of the politics of environmentalism and how this affects businesses. Increasingly, environmentalism as a political ideology is maturing. Environmentalists have produced a sociological, political, philosophical and economic literature of considerable depth and breadth. Its variety and power has certainly affected the political and administrative agendas of most of the nations of the world.

For some, environmentalism cannot be easily located on a left–right ideological spectrum. Some would prefer environmentalism to be politically neutral in a traditional sense. But a position of political neutrality lacks power and risks leaving in place not only the present relative distribution of economic benefits but also the present distribution of political power. Moreover any attempt to remain neutral is fraught with difficulties. For example the policy held by many environmentalists aimed at reducing the length of time spent at work is likely to have considerable gender repercussions with women facing the threat of being forced back into the home. Such a neutral stance is therefore likely to be branded as rather more conservative than anything else.

Many business managers doubtless find even centrist forms of environmentalism as indistinguishable from any other kind of left-wing radicalism. And perhaps there is more truth in that observation than some environmentalists would wish to admit. It is certainly the case that environmentalism challenges conservatism but just why some managers see that as a threat is rather more confusing. Management attitudes consistent with 'business as usual' and a strong individualist perspective on society provide some of the answers. But many more are to be found in a worrying inertia which is often associated with the management of modern enterprises (particularly when these are large-scale enterprises). Management needs to develop a much more critical perspective along with an injection of much-needed creativity.

Environmentalism as an ideology and as practical politics can adopt an eclectic and pragmatic view of policy tools. However, it is clearly distinguishable from conservatism and perhaps this is why conservatism has been consistently hostile to environmentalism in every country in which it has emerged. According to Paehlke (1989) environmentalists can distinguish themselves from conservatives in six different ways. Firstly, environmentalists would enhance rather than inhibit environmental regulation and enforcement. Secondly, they would oppose expansions in military spending. Thirdly, environmentalists would not make economic growth a high policy priority. Fourthly, they would tend whenever possible to increase expenditures on education, social welfare, the arts and health. Fifthly, they would systematically increase government revenue in a number of ways, and lastly, they would not treat the market economy as an individual sacred cow. In addition, environmentalists are much more likely to support enhanced opportunities for women and minorities.

## TOWARDS THE TRANSCENDENT ORGANISATION

For businesses to move towards sustainable development their managers and the institutions themselves have to take on board the ideology of environmentalism and this requires a rejection of conservatism. Environmentalism has always attached great importance to the development of participation and so the business organisation must become increasingly participatory. It must therefore adopt a scale in which participation can flourish. Environmentalists would also put great emphasis on decentralisation and regionalism and businesses need to consider their own structures and how these can be compatible with a move towards devolved decision-making, demergers and industrial compartmentalisation.

An orientation to an environmentally sustainable future therefore requires the transcendent organisation to grasp the political dimensions of environmentalism and act on these as well as on the economic and social aspects. The business must therefore be an important actor in the social mobilisation required to achieve the necessary adjustments in the habits of day-to-day living. These sorts of changes cannot be imposed from above; they require enthusiastic support from all economic agents. Such willingness, in turn, requires an understanding of the huge costs associated with the avoidance of change and the continuation of 'business as usual'.

The transcendent organisation is therefore one which is able to transcend the limited ideologies and values associated with traditional forms of environmental management. It will embrace ideals and policies more in keeping with deep ecology perspectives and will be ever mindful of sustainable development, widely defined. It will reject dominant management paradigms associated with environmental management systems as not going far enough and it will institute change consistent with ecological management practices. The transcendent organisation will audit for sustainability and introduce wide-ranging culture change programmes to make the values and actions of the firm consistent with sustainable development. It will reject conservatism and views associated with 'business as usual' and it will play a full part in educating consumers and campaigning for change through its green marketing strategies.

The transcendent organisation will not of course appear overnight. It will take time to change traditional management ideology and train a new breed of management. Moving the business organisation on to a sustainable track is fraught with difficulties especially when the present path seems increasingly to move us in the opposite direction and towards a self-destruct mechanism. We must challenge conventional 'wisdoms' and therefore, as a minimum, the organisation, its management and its workforce must begin to consider a radical agenda for change.

## AGENDA FOR CHANGE

Whilst it must be accepted that firms will not be able to act in strict accordance with sustainable development overnight, it is possible to set out an agenda for change which will challenge businesses to begin to consider the many aspects of their organisation which will need to be changed. Organisations need to transcend the traditional boundaries which force them into narrow 'business as usual' scenarios and they need to take consumers with them. This book ends therefore not with the normal all-embracing conclusion, but with a checklist for action expressed in terms of values, the organisation of industry, human and animal rights, and environmental strategy. It is a checklist which encompasses the approaches of deep ecology, of ecological management and of sustainable development. In no particular order, it is a checklist which could make the transcendent organisation a reality for the next millennium and a checklist which is fully consistent with the aims of Agenda 21 and sustainable development.

## Values

### The environment

The environment must be valued as an integral part of the economic process and not treated as a free good. The environmental stock has to be protected and this implies minimal use of non-renewable resources and minimal emission of pollutants. Ecosystems have to be protected and the loss of plant and animal species has to be avoided. All businesses must have a clear and unequivocal commitment to environmental improvement.

### Equity

One of the biggest threats facing the world is that the developing countries want to grow rapidly to achieve the same standards of living as those in the West. That in itself would cause a major environmental disaster if it were modelled on the same sort of growth experienced in post-war Europe. There therefore needs to be a greater degree of equity and the key issue of poverty has to be addressed. But equity, widely defined, is also about equality and a sustainable strategy must consider the inequalities inherent in modern society and begin to tackle issues such as the distribution of income and wealth and widespread discrimination.

*Futurity*

Sustainable development requires that society, businesses and individuals operate on a different timescale than currently operates in the economy. Whilst companies commonly operate under competitive pressures to achieve short run gains, long term environmental protection is often compromised. To ensure that longer term, intergenerational considerations are observed, longer planning horizons need to be adopted and business policy needs to be proactive rather than reactive in response to a recognition that the environment is a dynamic and not a static entity.

*Biodiversity*

Biological diversity is valuable for ecological, genetic, social, economic, recreational and aesthetic reasons. It is important for evolution and for maintaining the life-sustaining systems of the biosphere. Organisations must play their part in maintaining variability amongst living organisms. A full and proper respect of all living things is therefore an important element in any business strategy.

## The organisation of industry

*Scale*

Rather than putting an emphasis on optimum size in terms of how big an organisation can grow we ought to think about optimum smallness as well. Principles such as minimal ecological intrusiveness, control over resource use, worker participation, shared decision making and community involvement put limits on the extent to which an enterprise can grow. Traditional notions of economies of scale are only relevant where the environment is considered as a free resource and where large scale is appropriate to materialism and consumerism. None of these out-moded notions are compatible with sustainable development.

*Decentralisation*

Local action must be one of the main driving forces which will bring about global change. The business should play its full part in a strategy of decentralisation of decision making to incorporate wider worker participation and democratic structures. It must support local initiatives and be prepared to serve local niche markets rather than produce generic standardised products.

## Regionalism and bioregionalism

Industry can benefit greatly from the additional help which will be provided by firms working together cooperatively with the support of a regional team. There is a need, however, to go beyond traditional approaches to regional development and consider the concept of bioregionalism. This represents a vehicle for achieving sustainable development based on local organisation, and the business organisation should consider strategies associated with de-merger, post-Fordist production and organisation on a small-scale satellite basis.

## Employment and unemployment

Employment is a fundamental human right and as such unemployment must be eliminated in a move towards a full employment economy. If the organisation of society through capitalism cannot provide for full employment then that organisation must be changed. Unemployment is a massive waste of resources, leads to many social problems and is dehumanising for the individual. Firms need to look to their own employment policies, patterns and practices to increase their efforts to return to a full employment economy. Full employment may mean everyone working fewer hours or the replacement of technology with human power. It may mean a new emphasis put on local economic development and moves towards self-sufficiency in regions. Business must nevertheless accept its responsibility for protecting employment and employment rights.

## Human and animal rights

### Women

Women have an important role to play in society and their exploitation by businesses must be avoided. Equal pay for equal work, proper maternity arrangements and career breaks should be guaranteed. The role of women in helping us to move towards sustainable development is hampered by lack of access to senior management jobs and societal conditioning which prevents them, through poor education and life experiences, making a positive contribution. Businesses must value women more highly, ensure their representation at all levels of the organisation and encourage their participation in decision making.

## Minority rights

Minority groups have traditionally been exploited in society and their experiences of such exploitation has led many to withdraw from mainstream participation in business. Business should have positive discrimination policies which protect all minority groups. They should have clear published policies on the rights of minority groups and this should be enshrined in action for equal opportunities. Minority groups should not live in fear of expressing their diverse cultures, religious and other beliefs, sexual orientations and non-mainstream lifestyles. Businesses should provide for the emancipation of minorities.

## Equal opportunity

Businesses should ensure that all individuals regardless of any particular characteristic have equal access to all opportunities within the organisation. Strongly enforced equal opportunities policies should ensure that all workers are able fully to participate in the activities of the organisation. Where relevant, organisation should follow positive discrimination procedures to ensure that women and minority groups are fairly represented at all levels of the organisation.

## Rights of indigenous populations

Dominant ideologies in the First World aimed at the maximisation of profits and international trading relationships destroy traditional ways of living of Third World populations and are inconsistent with sustainable development. Indigenous people, who represent a significant part of the world's population, depend on renewable resources and ecosystems to maintain their well-being. Businesses should help to protect the fundamental rights of these people.

## Animal rights

Animal rights have long been a part of a wider ecological dimension which businesses must recognise. Ecological ethics should embrace all sentient beings. Business strategy should, as a minimum, include consideration of the impact on animals and, in particular, not allow animal testing as a base criterion. This is an approach which would be consistent with political and social reality and the views of consumers. Environmental strategies which ignore the wider issues of animal rights, endangered species and biodiversity will be incomplete and flawed.

# Environmental strategy

## Culture change

The culture of every organisation and each part of it needs to consider sustainable development. Each person needs to assess their contribution to ecological improvement and the organisation as a whole must introduce value-change programmes which add to this process. Systemic management must be at the heart of the culture change programme along with greater emphasis placed on worker participation, shared decision making and workplace democracy.

## Ecological management

Traditional approaches to environmental management provide a direction in which the organisation must move but they do not go far enough. The principles of ecological management, which include the introduction of full life cycle assessment for all products, a dynamic approach to environmental auditing and a fuller consideration of the organisation's impact on ecosystems, need to be firmly embedded in the organisation's corporate strategy.

## Auditing for sustainability

Businesses must undertake environmental audits based not on the principles of management systems but on the fundamental principle of sustainable development. Auditing for sustainability requires firms to look at their overall impact on the environment (widely defined), on equity and on futurity. It challenges firms to prioritise their actions in ecological terms rather than management systems terms. Businesses ought to place more emphasis on auditing products and processes and therefore there is a central emphasis on the need for life cycle assessment.

## Product assessment

Products should all be assessed using a full life cycle assessment approach. For products currently under production, firms should look towards new design, product stewardship campaigns and help with the re-use, recycling and disposal of that product, in order to improve its environmental performance. New product development should at all times internalise the full ecological impacts of its whole life cycle. Part of any product profile must include environmental education and advice on use and disposal for the consumer.

## Environmental information

Environmental information and the establishment of comprehensive environmental information systems will be central to any organisation committed to moving towards sustainability. Moreover, that information must be freely available to anyone who wishes to see it. Environmental strategy must be based on openness, honesty and credibility and therefore organisations must be able to prove and justify all their actions through the provision of environmental information to third parties.

## Green marketing, campaigning and education

At the centre of any green marketing strategy there must be a shift away from cynical forms of product promotion, sales hype and stereotypical advertising. An ethical approach to the marketing function will involve imparting honest and open information to the consumer and playing a full part in the environmental education of the consumer. The organisation committed to sustainable development will also make a contribution to campaigns for change helping to push forward the frontiers of environmental action.

# BIBLIOGRAPHY

Ansoff, H. I. (1979) 'The changing shape of the strategic problem', in Schendel, D. and Hofer, C. (Eds), *Strategic Management: A New View of Business Policy and Planning* (pp. 30–44), Little, Brown, Boston.

Argyris, C. (1964) *Integrating the Individual and the Organisation*, John Wiley, New York.

Bahro, R. (1986) *Building the Green Movement*, GMP, London.

Bartunek, J. M. and Moch, M. K. (1987) 'First-order, second-order, and third-order change and organisation development interventions: a cognitive approach', *Journal of Applied Behavioural Science* 23, 483–500.

Bennis, W. (1972) 'A funny thing happened on the way to the future', in Thomas, J. and Bennis, W. (Eds), *The Management of Change and Conflict*, Penguin Books, Harmondsworth.

Brown, L. (1991) 'The new world order', in Brown, L. *et al.*, *State of the World 1991*, Earthscan, London.

Burke, T., Maddock, S. and Rose, A. (1993) 'How ethical is British business?', Research Working Paper, Series 2, Number 1, University of Westminster.

Burns, T. and Stalker, G. (1963) *The Management of Innovation*, Tavistock Press, London.

Burrows, B., Mayne, A. and Newbury, P. (1991), *Into the 21st Century. A Handbook for a Sustainable Future*, Adamantine, Twickenham.

Callenbach, E., Capra, F., Goldman, L., Lutz, R. and Marburg, S. (1993) *EcoManagement: The Elmwood Guide to Ecological Auditing and Sustainable Business*, Berrett-Koehler Publishers, San Fransisco.

Cannon, T. (1993) *How To Get Ahead In Business*, Virgin, London.

Carley, M. and Christie, I. (1992) *Managing Sustainable Development*, Earthscan, London.

Carson, R. (1965) *Silent Spring*, Penguin, Harmondsworth.

Cavanagh, G., Moberg, D. and Valasquez, M. (1981) 'The ethics of organisational politics', *Academy of Management Review* 6(3), 363–374.

Coddington, W. (1993) *Environmental Marketing: Positive Strategies for Reaching the Green Consumer*, McGraw Hill, New York.

Commission of the European Communities (1991) 'Europe 2000: Outlook for the Development of the Community's Territory', Communication from the Commission to the Council and the European Parliament, Brussels.

Commoner, B. (1990) 'Can capitalists be environmentalists?', *Business and Society Review* 75, 31–35.

Cosgrove, D. (1990) 'Environmental thought and action: pre-modern and post-modern', *Transactions of the Institute of British Geographers* 15, 3.

Daly, H. E. and Cobb, J. B., Jr (1989) *For the Common Good*, Beacon, Boston.

Deal, T. E. and Kennedy, A. A. (1982) *Corporate Cultures*, Addison-Wesley, New York.

Deci, E. L. and Ryan, R. M. (1985) *Intrinsic Motivation and Self-Determination in Human Behaviour*, Plenum, New York.

Derrida, J. (1978) *Writing and Difference*, Routledge & Kegan Paul, London.

DiMaggio, P. J. and Powell, W. (1983) 'The iron cage revisited: institutional isomorphism and collective rationale in organisational fields', *American Sociological Review* 48, 147–160.

Dodge, J., Nixon, O. and Welford, R. (1993) 'Research into environmental value congruence and integration', *Proceedings of the 1993 Business Strategy and the Environment Conference*, Bradford.

Dodwell, D. (1992) 'Environment better served by free trade carrot than protectionist stick', *Financial Times*, May 13.

Donaldson, J. (1989) *Key Issues in Business Ethics*, Academic Press Inc, San Diego.

Donaldson, J. and Waller, M. (1980) 'Ethics and organisation', *Journal of Management Studies* 17, 1.

Drambo, L. (1988) 'The futures circle', *Social Inventions* 11.

Drucker, P. F. (1973) *Management: Tasks, Responsibilities, Practices*, Harper & Row, New York.

Durning, A. (1991) 'Asking how much is enough', in Brown, L. *et al.*, *State of the World 1991*, Earthscan, London.

Dyllik, T., (1989) 'Ökologisch bewußte Unternehmungsführung: Der Beitrag der Managementlehre', Swiss Association for Ecologically Conscious Management, St Gallen.

Ekins, P. (Ed.) (1986) *The Living Economy*, Routledge & Kegan Paul, London.

Elkington, J. and Burke, T. (1987) *The Green Capitalists*, Gollancz, London.

Environmental Data Services (ENDS) (1993a) 'Many companies slow to commit resources to BS 7750', *ENDS* 216, January.

Environmental Data Services ENDS (1993b) 'Pitfalls still ahead for BS 7750', *ENDS* 218, March.

Environmental Data Services (ENDS) (1993c) 'Jury still out on responsible care', Industry report no. 55, *ENDS* 222, July.

Engel, J. R. and Engel, J. G. (1990) 'The ethics of sustainable development', in Engel, J. R. and Engel, J. G., *Ethics of Environment and Development: Global Challenge*, International Response, Belhaven, London.

EPA (1993) 'Status Report on the Use of Environmental Labels Worldwide', Report prepared by Abt Associates for the US Environmental Protection Agency, Washington DC.

Ernst, K. R. and Baginski, R. M. (1989/1990) 'Visioning: the key to effective strategic planning', in Glass, H. E. (Ed.), *Handbook of Business Strategy* (chap. 22), Warren, Gorham & Lamont, Boston.

Etzioni, A. (1991) 'What community, what responsiveness?', *The Responsive Community* 2(1), 5–8.

Fabrycky, W. J. and Blanchard, B. S. (1991) *Life Cycle Cost and Economic Analysis*, Prentice-Hall, New York.

Farnham, A. (1991), 'What comes after greed?', *Fortune* 14 January, 43–44.

Faulkner, M. J. (1980) 'Older workers and the transition to retirement', Commission of the European Communities.

Fleming, D. (1992) 'The Fifth EC Environmental Action Programme', European Environment, Special Supplement.

Freeman, R. E. and Gilbert, D. R., Jr (1988) *Corporate Strategy and the Search for Ethics*, Prentice-Hall, Englewood Cliffs, NJ.

Friedman, M. (1963) *Capitalism and Freedom*, Phoenix Books, University of Chicago Press, Chicago.

Gatenby, D. A. and Foo, G. (1990) 'Design for X: the key to competitive and profitable markets', *AT&T Technical Journal* 69 (2).

Gergen, K. (1992) 'Organisation Theory in the Postmodern Era', in Reed, M. and Hughes, M., *Rethinking Organisation*, Sage, London.

Gilbert, M. (1994) 'BS7750 and the eco-management and audit Regulation', *Eco-management and Auditing* 1 (2).

Gladwin, T. N. (1993) 'The meaning of greening: a plea for organizational theory', in Fischer, K. and Schott, J. (Eds) *Environmental Strategies for Industry*, Island Press, Washington DC.

Halal, W. E. (1986) *The New Capitalism*, John Wiley & Sons, New York.

Hall, S. and Jacques, M. (Eds) (1989) *New Times: The Changing Face of Politics in the 1990s*, Lawrence & Wishart, London.

Hartley, R. F. (1993) *Business Ethics: Violations of the Public Trust*, Wiley, New York.

Harvey, D. (1989) *The Condition of Postmodernity*, Blackwell, Oxford.

Hassard, J. and Parker, M. (Eds) (1993) *Postmodernism and Organisations*, Sage, London.

Heisenberg, W. (1985) 'Scientific and religious truths', in Wilber, K. (Ed.), *Quantum Questions* (pp. 39–44), New Science Library, Boston.

Hemming, C. (1992) 'Eco-labelling of washing machines: a UK pilot survey', *Integrated Environmental Management* 1 (2).

Hindle, P. and Payne, A. G. (1991) 'Value impact', *The Chemical Engineer* 31 (3).

Hirsch, F. (1977) *Social Limits to Growth*, Routledge & Kegan Paul, London.

Hoe, S. (1978), *The Man who Gave his Companies' Power Away*, Heinemann, London.

Holloway, R. J. and Hancock, R. S. (1968) *Marketing in a Changing Environment*, Wiley, New York.

International Chamber of Commerce (1989) *A Guide to Environmental Auditing*, ICC, London.

IUCN, UNEP, WWF (1991) *Caring for the Earth. A Strategy for Sustainable Living*, Gland, Switzerland.

Javeau, C. (1980) *Old Age and Retirement*, Commission of the European Communities.

Jungk, R. and Mullert, N. (1987) *Future Workshops - How to Create Desirable Futures*, Institute for Social Interventions, London.

Koestler, A. (1964) *The Act of Creation*, Hutchinson, London.

Kohr, L. (1957) *The Breakdown of Nations*, Routledge & Kegan Paul, London.

Kok, E., O'Laoire, D. and Welford, R. J. (1993) 'Environmental management at the regional level. A case study: the Avoca-Avonmore catchment conversion project', *Journal of Environmental Planning and Management* 36 (3).

Kotler, P. (1984) *Marketing Management: Analysis, Planning and Control*, Prentice-Hall, New York.

Luthans, F. (1985) *Organisational Behaviour* (4th edn), McGraw Hill, New York.

Lutz, R. (1990) 'The development of ecologically conscious management in Germany', Global File Report 1, Elmwood Institute, Berkeley, California.

Mayne, A. J. (1965) 'Creativity, psi and human personality', *Research Journal of Philosophy and Social Sciences*, 2 (1).

Milbrath, L. W. (1989) *Envisioning a Sustainable society*, State University of New York Press, Albany.

Mintzberg, H. (1979) *The Structuring of Organisations*, Prentice-Hall, New York.

Montaigne, M. de (1958a) 'On the education of children', in Cohen, J. M. (trans.), *Michel de Montaigne Essays* (pp. 60–65), Penguin, Harmondsworth (original work published in 1580).

Montaigne, M. de (1958b), 'That one man's profit is another's loss', in Cohen, J. M. (trans.), *Michel de Montaigne Essays* (pp. 48–53), Penguin, Harmondsworth (original work published 1580).

Morgan, G. (1986) *Images of Organisations*, Sage, Newbury Park, CA.

Ochse, R. (1990) *Before the Gates of Excellence – the Determinants of Creative Genius*, Cambridge University Press, Cambridge and New York.

Ornstein, R. and Ehrlich, P. (1990) *New World, New Mind*, Touchstone, New York.

Paehlke, R. C. (1989) *Environmentalism and the Future of Progressive Politics*, Yale University Press, New Haven.

Pearce, D. W. and Turner, R. K. (1990) *Economics of Natural Resources and the Environment*, Harvester Wheatsheaf, UK.

Peattie, K. (1992) *Green Marketing*, M & E Handbooks, Pitman Publishing, London.

Pepper, D. (1993) *Eco-socialism: from Deep Ecology to Social Justice*, Routledge, London.

Peters, T. (1990) 'Prometheus barely unbound', *Academy of Management Executive* 4(4), 70–84.

Peters, T. J., and Waterman, R. H., Jr (1982) *In Search of Excellence*, Harper & Row, New York.

Piore, M. and Sabel, C. (1984) *The Second Industrial Divide*, Basic Books, New York.

Plant, J. (1987) *Managing Change and Making it Stick*, Fontana, London.

Post, J. E. and Altman, B. (1991) 'Corporate Environmentalism: The Challenge of Organisational Learning', National Academy of Management Meeting, Miami, Fl.

Power, M. (1990) 'Modernism, postmodernism and organisations', in Hassard, J. and Pym, D. (Eds), *The Theory and Philosophy of Organisations*, Routledge, London.

Rickards, T. (1974) *'Problem Solving Through Creative Analysis*, Gower Press, Epping, Essex.

Roome, N. (1992) 'Developing environmental management strategies', *Business Strategy and the Environment* (1) 1.

Rose, F. (1990) 'A new age for business?', *Fortune*, October 8, pp. 156–164.

Sale, K. (1974) 'Mother of all', in Kumar, S. (Ed.), *The Schumacher Lectures, Vol. 2*, Abacus, London.

Sale, K. (1985) *Dwellers in the Land: the Bioregional Vision*, Sierra Club, San Francisco.

Sarkar, S. (1983) 'Marxism and productive forces: a critique', *Alternatives*, IX.

Schein, E. H. (1985) *Organisational Culture and Leadership*, Jossey-Bass, San Francisco.

Schumacher, E. F. (1973) *Small is Beautiful: Economics as if People Mattered*, Harper & Row, New York.

Schumacher, E. F. (1974) *Small is Beautiful*, Abacus, London.

Schumacher, E. F. (1979) *Good Work*, Harper & Row, New York.

Scmidheiny, S. (1992) *Changing Course*, MIT Press, Boston, Ma.

Senge, P. M. (1990) *The Fifth Discipline: The Art and Practice of the Learning Organisation*, Doubleday/Currency, New York.

Shayler, M., Welford, R. J. and Shayler, G. (1994) 'BS7750: panacea or palliative?', *Eco-management and Auditing* 1 (2).

Speth, G. (1990) 'The crucial decade: environmental imperatives for the 1990s', in *Proceedings of the Business Week Symposium on the Environment: Corporate Stewardship & Business Opportunity in the Decade of Global Awakening* (pp. 1–4), Journal Graphics, New York.

Stead, W. E. and Stead, J. E. (1992) *Management for a Small Planet*, Sage Publications, Newbury Park.

Steward, F. (1989) 'Green times', in Hall, S. and Jacques, M. (Eds), *New Times: The Changing Face of Politics in the 1990s*, Lawrence & Wishart, London.

Tokars, B. (1987) *The Green Alternative*, R & E Miles, San Pedro, California.

UNDP (1992) *Human Development Report 1992*, Oxford University Press, Oxford.

UNEP (1991) 'Global Environmental Labelling: Invitational Expert Seminar, Lesvos, Greece', United Nations Environment Programme/IEO Cleaner Production Programme, New York.

Van Berkel, R. *et al.* (1991) 'Business examples with waste prevention: ten case studies from the Dutch PRISMA project', in *Prepare for Tomorrow*, Ministry for Economic Affairs, The Netherlands.

Welford, R. J. (1989) 'Growth and the performance-participation nexus: the case of U.K. producer cooperatives', *Economic Analysis and Workers' Management* 23.

Welford, R. J. (1992) 'Linking Quality and the Environment', *Business Strategy and the Environment* 1 (1).

Welford, R. J. (1993) 'Local Economic Development and Environmental Management: An Integrated Approach', *Local Economy* 8 (2).

Welford, R. J. (1994a) 'Management Systems and Environmental Disasters' in Welford, R. J., *Cases in Environmental Management and Business Strategy*, Pitman Publishing, London.

Welford, R. J. (1994b) *Cases in Environmental Management and Business Strategy*, Pitman Publishing, London.

Welford, R. J. and Gouldson, A. P. (1993) *Environmental Management and Business Strategy*, Pitman Publishing, London.

Welford, R. J. and Prescott, C. E. (1994) *European Business: an Issue Based Approach*, Pitman Publishing, London.

Westing, J. H. (1968) 'Some thoughts on the nature of ethics in marketing', in Mayer, R. (Ed.), *Marketing Systems, 1967 Winter Conference Proceedings*, Marketing Association, Chicago.

Wheeler, D. (1993a) 'Auditing for sustainability: philosophy and practice of The Body Shop International, *Eco-management and Auditing* 1 (1).

Wheeler, D. (1993b) 'Why human and animal rights matter in ecological policy making in Europe', paper presented to the Club de Bruxelles Conference on Eco-auditing and Eco-labelling in Europe, Brussels, November.

Wheeler, D. (1994) 'Auditing for sustainability: philosophy and practice of The Body Shop International', in *Environmental, Health and Safety Auditing Handbook*, McGraw-Hill, Ma.

Winsemius, P. and Guntram, U. (1992) 'Responding to the environmental challenge', *Business Horizons* (2), 38–45.

Winter, G. (1987) *Das umweltbewusste Unternehmen (Business and the Environment)* Becksche Verlagsbuchhandlung, Munich.

World Commission on Environment and Development (1987) *Our Common Future*, Oxford University Press, Oxford.

Zenisek, T. J. (1979) 'Corporate social responsibility: a conceptualisation based on organisational literature', *Academy of Management Review* 4(2), 359–368.

# INDEX

*Note: Emboldened references denote chapters.*

Environmental Choice
Programme 169
capitalism 13, 14, 23, 28, 188,
189–90; reform 2–3
Capra, F. 80, 83, 86, 93, 114–15,
117–18, 147, 150, 164
Carley, M. 13–14
Carson, Rachel, *Silent Spring* 1–2
Cavanagh, G. 127
certification *see* environmental
certification programmes
Chemical Industries Association
(CIA) 35–6
chemical industry 35–7
Chernobyl disaster 150
Christie, I. 13–14
circular relationships 143
Cobb, J. B. 132, 138, 139, 145
Coddington, W. 152
codes of conduct *see* ethics
cognitive structures 120
collectivism *see* cooperation
Commoner, B. 87
communications 157, 161–4;
strategy 150–1; technology and
networks 15–16
communities 116, 137–9, 145–6,
186; liaison groups 36; size 185
competition 22, 40, 43, 154, 184;
strategies 12
compliance audits 56, 83
conservation 131
conservatism 197
consultancies, audit 58–9
consumers 11, 14–19, 59, 150,
162–3, 166; and business ethics
33; and environmental
performance 195–6; interests 41;
needs 144–5; protection 167;
purchasing survey 172;
satisfaction 54–5, 143; in USA
150
consumption 5, 7, 9; and marketing
15–16; USA 15; and work
satisfaction 140
cooperation 22, 44, 145–6, 154, 178,
179; strategies 12, 40
corporations: culture defined 114;
objectives 11–12, 52, 64;

philosophy and relationships
32–3; policy 155; strategies
6–12, 76, 127; and sustainable
development 10–12;
transnational 12–13, 16; *see also*
auditing; management;
performance
Cosgrove, D. 186
costs 59; environmental 17, 89, 177,
182; reduction 43, 57, 140
creativity 81, 92, 144
culture: barriers 119–21; change
21–2, 43–4, **114–48**, 141, 203;
control 16

Daly, H. E. 132, 138, 139, 145
Deal, T. E. 121
decentralisation 24, 132, 197–8,
200–1; *see also* bioregionalism
Deci, E. L. 116
decision-making 47, 53, 116, 118,
132, 135–6, 137, 200–1; criteria
142–7
democracy: industrial 46–7; in
workplace 10, 42, 128–31, 200–1
development *see* sustainable
development
Derrida, J. 24
design of products 88–9, 101, 103;
of cricket ball 107–8; and
government 166
devolution *see* decentralisation
DiMaggio, P. J. 41
discrimination 130, 202
distribution 156
Dodge, J. 116
Dodwell, D. 182
Donaldson, J. 30, 31, 34–5, 43
Drambo, L. 144
Drucker, P. F. 149
dualism 23–4
Durning, A. 16
Dyllik, T. 81

Earth Summit, Rio de Janeiro 123
Earth's age 136–7
eco-anarchists 186
eco-labelling 7, 37–8, 59, 102,
164–72; benefits 171–2; product

Friedman, M. 39
Friends of the Earth 178
futurity 8, 101, 137–8, 200

Gatenby, D. A. 101
GE 126
General Agreement of Tariffs and
  Trade (GATT) 14
Gergen, K. 25
Germany 164
Gilbert, D. R. 120, 126–7
Gilbert, M. 74
Gladwin, T. N. 19
global values 117, 121–4
Goldman, L. 80, 83, 86, 93, 114–15,
  117–18, 147, 150, 164
Gouldson, A. P. 5, 50, 65–6, 79,
  93–4
government 166, 195–6
green movement 19–22, **149–73**,
  192–3; advertising and marketing
  16, 45, 59, 153–7, 204; imagery
  163–4
Greenland 131
Gross National Product (GNP)
  8–9
growth: economic 5, 7, 8–9, 13–14,
  39–40; hard 128; smart 127–8;
  sustainable 122; of wealth 16–17
Guntram, U. 182

Hancock, R. S. 40
Halal, W. E. 126, 127–8
Hall, S., *New Times* 25
hard growth 128
Hartley, R. F. 28, 32, 38, 40, 43
Harvey, D. 24
Hassard, J. 24
health and safety *see* BSI
health-and-safety-type audits 84
Heisenberg, W. 138
Hemming, C. 104
Hindle, P. 107
Hirsch, F. 16
holistic planning 95–6; auditing
  84–6, 87–90; management 147;
  philosophy 128–9; systemic
  thinking 142–7
Holloway, R. J. 40

human rights 126–7, 129, 171,
  201–3

imagery: of business 32–3; of green
  movement 163–4; public 57
indigenous populations 183, 202
individual values 117, 131–41
individualism 15; radical 138
industrial development 187
inflation 134
information 157–61
insurance 59
interdependence 12, 82, 116, 147,
  178
International Chamber of
  Commerce: audit defined 86
International Monetary Fund
  (IMF) 13
international standards on EMS 63
international trade 12–14, 45–6
inventories 67–8, 112; definition
  105
investment: REMS 182
Ireland 63
Iroquois Indians 137
ISO9000 *see* BS5750

Jacques, M., *New Times* 25
Japan 12, 140, 164; EcoMark
  programme 169–70
Javeau, C. 129
Jungk, R. 144

Kennedy, A. A. 121
Koestler, A. 144
Kohr, L. 184
Kok, E. 187
Kotler, P. 149

labelling *see* eco-labelling
Laing, Martin 125–6
Landskrona project, Sweden 179
language 31, 120
law: environmental protection 11;
  and ethics 38; European 59–60;
  labelling 165–6; legislation 10,
  56, 57, 58, 88, 91–2; in USA
  59–60
leadership, key points 93

Coventry University

217